FOUND YOUR ONE THING
YET? ABSOLUTELY NOT!

Found Your One Thing Yet? Absolutely Not!

MAGGIE O'HARA

Contents

Dedication		vi
	Forward	1
	Introduction	3
	My Multi-passionate soul	5
	A Note from the Author	6
	FOUR SECTIONS	7
	SECTION 1	9
1	Finding My One Thing	10
2	Exploring systems for busy minds	17
	SECTION 2	21
3	Empower Yourself	22
4	E. EXPLORE	26
5	M. MANIFEST	33
6	P. PRIORITISE	42
7	O. ORGANISE	51
8	W. WEAVE	60
9	E. EMPOWER	69
10	R. REFLECT	78

	SECTION 3	87
11	STRATEGIES AND ACTIONS	88
12	OVERCOMING CHALLENGES	98
13	COMMUNITY AND SUPPORT	106
14	STRATEGIES FOR CREATIVES	116
15	CONCLUSION	126
	SECTION 4	129
16	JOURNAL ACTIVITY 01	130
17	JOURNAL ACTIVITY 02	134
18	JOURNAL ACTIVITY 03	140
19	JOURNAL ACTIVITY 04	144
20	JOURNAL ACTIVITY 05	146
21	JOURNAL ACTIVITY 06	148
22	JOURNAL ACTIVITY 06	150
23	JOURNAL ACTIVITY 07	152
24	JOURNAL ACTIVITY 08	154
25	JOURNAL ACTIVITY 09	156
26	JOURNAL ACTIVITY 10	158
27	WHAT NEXT?	160

About the Author	165
Other Books by the Author	167

Copyright © 2025 by Maggie O'Hara
All rights reserved. No part of this book may be reproduced in any manner whatsoever without written permission except in the case of brief quotations embodied in critical articles and reviews.
First Printing, 2025 Butterfly Grove Press
Printed in Australia

For more information or to book an event, contact :
info@maggieoharas.com
http://www.maggieoharas.com

Cover design by Maggie O'Hara

ISBN paperback 978-0-6480513-5-0

Publisher: Butterfly Grove Press

Dedicated to my two daughters

To Caitlin and Sophie

You are the constant stars in my ever-changing sky. This book is a testament to the strength you've instilled in me. May you be confident in your ability to pursue multiple passions.

Forward

Have you ever felt overwhelmed by the idea of choosing just one path in life? For those of us with many interests and passions, the pressure to focus on a single direction can feel restrictive, like we're being asked to cut off pieces of ourselves to fit into a world that often values simplicity over complexity.

I'm excited to introduce you to this book by Maggie O'Hara. It's a guide for anyone who has struggled to make sense of their many passions or felt torn between the things that bring them joy. Maggie brings her unique voice, deep understanding, and years of experience to this work, offering readers a way to embrace their multifaceted nature with intention and clarity.

This book is a celebration of being multi-passionate, a reminder that having a variety of interests isn't a flaw, but a gift. Maggie doesn't shy away from the challenges that come with it, like self-doubt, the fear of feeling scattered, or societal expectations to focus on just one thing. Instead, she tackles these struggles head-on, offering practical advice, insightful reflections, and actionable steps to help you turn what might feel like chaos into a meaningful and fulfilling life.

One of the standout elements of this book is the EMPOWER method: Explore, Manifest, Prioritise, Organise, Weave, Empower, and Reflect. This practical framework provides a clear path for navigating your many interests, setting priorities, and aligning your passions with your goals. It's more than just a set of tools, it's a way of thinking that encourages you to embrace who you are and build momentum toward the life you want.

What I appreciate most about Maggie's approach is how deeply it honours individuality. This book isn't about forcing you into a box or suggesting there's only one way to live. Instead, it gives you the freedom and support to chart your own course. Whether you're looking to make sense of your many passions, overcome the feeling of being pulled in too many directions, or create a practical plan for the future, Maggie's guidance will help you find your way.

This isn't about searching for a single true calling or narrowing yourself to fit the mould. It's about giving yourself permission to follow what makes you come alive and building a framework that supports your unique ambitions.

As you read, you'll find moments to pause, reflect, and take action. Take your time. Let Maggie's words challenge and inspire you, and let the exercises guide you toward clarity. This book isn't just a guide, it's a resource and a companion for the journey of embracing your multi-passionate self.

So, take a deep breath, turn the page, and get ready to embark on a journey of self-discovery, clarity, and empowerment. This is your time to embrace yourself.

Lydia C Saiz (Arbibo)

Introduction

Hey there, friend! I'm so glad you picked up this book, took a leap of faith, and journeyed alongside me. I'm not just saying that; I genuinely mean it. I know there are a million places you could be right now, a thousand books you could read. But here we are, ready to dive into this fantastic, messy, beautiful journey of being a multi-passionate person.

My name is Maggie, and before we go any further, let's clarify: I'm not an expert or someone who has all the answers. I'm just like you. People ask me, 'When will you find your one thing?' or 'Why can't you settle?'

This book introduces some systems developed by others and how I have created a simple method that makes sense to me. It is my journey of discovery, and I hope it helps you find some answers.

So, get ready for self-discovery, whether in your PJs, sipping coffee, or taking a break during a hectic workday. Your comfort is essential. We're about to dive deep into personal anecdotes, actionable steps, journal exercises, and activities to help you become the fantastic, multi-passionate person you were born to be.

Let's treat this as a safe space for self-discovery and empowerment for multi-passionate people. Before we get started, one more thing: this book isn't meant to be rushed. It's a journey, not a race. So, take your time. Digest it, soak it in, and reflect upon it. If something doesn't resonate with you, that's okay. Take what serves you, and leave what doesn't. Feel free to use different coloured highlighters to mark actions you like.

A couple of action steps are repeated in Chapters Two and Three, so you can look at them with different eyes. Re-do the activities and see if they reveal anything new when you do them again. There are over fifty action steps and strategies to assist you on your journey. I hope you're as excited to start this journey as I am. Grab a comfy spot, and let's get started. After all, the best time for a new beginning is now.

> **"Stay curious.
> The joy of discovery lies in exploring
> new interests and horizons."**

My Multi-passionate soul

In the heart of many dreams, a spark ignites,
A myriad of passions, dancing in the night.
Not bound by one path, nor a single frame,
You are the essence of a multi-passionate flame.

Like a river flowing, never still,
You chase the currents, guided by your will.
Each turn a new adventure, each twist a chance,
To learn, to grow, and to join the creative dance.

Fear not the whispers of perfection's call,
For in your journey, there's beauty in all.
Mistakes are but brushstrokes on life's grand canvas,
Each one a lesson, a step towards vastness.

So, embrace your journey, let your heart sing,
With the joy of many passions that only you bring.
In the dance of your soul, find your own rhyme,
You are a multi-passionate, limitless and sublime.

Maggie O'Hara

A Note from the Author

Embracing our multi-passionate nature is not just a choice; it's a celebration of who we are. Our diverse interests and talents are not distractions but the culmination of our life experiences, which tell our unique story.

We can blend, create, and innovate in ways that others may not see. Remember, pivoting, exploring, and embracing new ideas is okay. Each passion you pursue adds depth and richness to your life.

Your journey as a multi-passionate individual is a gift. It allows you to view the world broadly, connect seemingly unrelated dots, and offer fresh perspectives on everything you do.

So, continue to follow your excitement, trust in your unique path, and celebrate the vibrant, multifaceted individual you are.

With heartfelt encouragement,

Maggie O'Hara

FOUR SECTIONS

This book is broken into four sections, so you can jump ahead or read the relevant sections. This is not a library book; this is your copy to help you on your journey, so if you feel like highlighting tips or strategies you want to return to later, feel free to do so. Think of it more like a workbook or an ideas book.

Not everything may work or resonate with you. So take what you need and leave the rest.

Section One
Introduction to Multi-Passionate Living

Section Two
Introducing the EMPOWER method

Section Three
Developing strategies and action steps

Section Four
Mapping out your Life Blueprint activities

I AM
CONSTANTLY
GROWING AND
EVOLVING INTO
A BETTER
VERSION OF
MYSELF

SECTION 1

Introduction to Multi-Passionate Living

Chapter 1

Finding My One Thing

Does this sound familiar? You're overflowing with ideas, passions, and dreams, but instead of feeling inspired, you feel stuck. Stuck in indecision, trapped between too many possibilities, paralysed by the thought of choosing just one path. You hear the well-meaning advice of others—"just focus on one thing" or "find your niche"—and it feels like a betrayal of who you are.

Maybe you've felt the weight of external expectations, attempting to conform to a single label or path. You've been trying to specialise, to fit into a box, only to feel restless and disconnected. And in those moments when you give in to exploring your passions, guilt creeps in, whispering, "You're spreading yourself too thin. You'll never truly excel."

The outcome? Exhaustion, burnout, and self-doubt. You've tried self-help books, various strategies, and those "foolproof" systems to organise your life. Yet, they've only left you feeling more frustrated because they weren't tailored for someone like you—someone who thrives on diversity and creativity.

Now, imagine this: A life where your passions coexist harmoniously. A life where you wake up excited, knowing each day is filled with purpose and creativity. You've learned to integrate your multifaceted nature into a dynamic, fulfilling lifestyle—without sacrificing your authenticity or feeling pulled in every direction.

Instead of spinning in circles, you've found clarity. You've created a rhythm honouring your passions and aligning with your values. The pressure to "choose just one thing" has disappeared because you've discovered a way to make them all work together. This is your "Heaven Island"—a life of balance, joy, and empowerment.

Your Multi-Passionate Nature is Your Superpower

I've been where you are. I've pursued the "safe" career paths, taken self-help courses, and even pushed myself into hobbies that resonated with others but weren't fulfilling. None of it worked. It wasn't until I had an epiphany!

> "*My multi-passionate nature isn't a flaw; it's a strength.*"

Instead of resisting, I started to embrace it. I realised that my varied interests weren't distractions—they were assets.

By learning to honour and integrate my passions, I unlocked a life filled with creativity and joy. And you can, too.

This realisation inspired me to develop my EMPOWER Method, a step-by-step framework for multi-passionate individuals like us. It's not about narrowing your focus or choosing just one path; it's about creating a life that empowers you to pursue all your passions without burnout or guilt.

My Story

From a young age, I was always curious and eager to explore new things. As I grew older, my interests expanded. I took up cake decorating, delighting in the intricate designs I could create with icing and fondant. Photography became another passion, capturing moments of beauty and preserving them forever. Each new hobby brought a fresh wave of excitement and a sense of accomplishment.

One of the most fulfilling projects I completed was writing and illustrating my first children's book, "*Elly Rose Selfies from Townsville.*" The idea for the book came to me one evening while I was looking at photos from one of my adventures. Why not combine my love for writing, illustration, travel, and culture?

I completed the project in 12 months, from writing the story to creating the illustrations and learning the intricacies of self-publishing. Holding the finished book in my hands was one of the proudest moments of my life.

FOUND YOUR ONE THING YET? ABSOLUTELY NOT!

The following year, drawing on the experience from my first book, I refined the process and wrote four more children's books. Each book offered a fresh adventure, enabling me to explore different cultural themes and introduce new characters.

The joy I felt from seeing my ideas come to life on the pages was incredible. Each book brought a new wave of excitement and creativity, fuelling my passion and drive.

Managing various interests and projects can be challenging, but I have learned some techniques to maintain balance and prevent feeling overwhelmed.

My life has been wonderfully non-linear. Living in various places across Queensland and New South Wales and travelling to many countries has significantly shaped my multifaceted interests. Every new place exposed me to diverse cultures, ideas, and forms of artistic expression. These experiences enriched my creative concepts and offered endless inspiration for my projects.

Embracing diversity has brought immense joy and fulfilment to my life. I've created a dynamic and satisfying life by following my curiosity and allowing myself the freedom to explore diverse interests. This journey requires flexibility and mindfulness, but the rewards are worth the effort.

My journey as a multi-passionate is a testament to the power of embracing my true nature and celebrating the richness of a multifaceted life.

How I felt before the EMPOWER method.

Stuck in Indecision: I felt paralysed by too many choices. I had many passions but didn't know which one to focus on. I was spinning in circles, overwhelmed by the sheer number of possibilities.

Overwhelmed by Expectations: I grew tired of hearing the same advice: "Just pick one thing" or "Find your niche." However, that advice felt like a betrayal of who I was—a person who thrives on diversity, creativity, and exploration. For many years, the pressure from others made me question the validity of my way of life.

Doubting My Value: With so many passions pulling me in different directions, I questioned whether I was good enough at any of them. Family members would say, "You are spreading yourself too thin." I wondered if I would ever truly excel in any area because I was not fully committing to one path.

Burnt Out and Exhausted: Whenever I tried to focus on one passion or idea, another called my name. This cycle left me feeling drained and exhausted. I tried multiple strategies, systems, and self-help advice but needed more to achieve the clarity and focus I craved.

What I've Previously Tried

Forcing Specialisation: I tried to follow my parents' advice and concentrate on one thing. I chose sewing as a hobby and committed myself to learning as much as possible while making clothes for myself and my two young daughters. I hoped it would bring me the fulfilment I craved. I focused solely on being a mum. However, after some time, I began to feel restless and disconnected. I started to miss my other passions, and before I realised it, I was once again caught in boredom and restlessness.

Self-Help Books or Courses: I've taken numerous courses, read various books, and followed mentors who promised clarity and purpose. However, their advice often fell short because it was tailored for individuals with a singular focus. While I found temporary motivation, none of these solutions helped me embrace my multi-passionate nature.

I've tried to meet other people's expectations by choosing a career path that felt "safe" or "practical." I entered the banking industry hoping it would suffice, but deep down, it left me feeling unfulfilled. The passions I'd set aside for stability still called out to me. I explored many careers (11+) and never really found "my thing."

Combining the EMPOWER Method, journal prompts, and the activities in this book offers a solution. Together, they help you organise, prioritise, and, most importantly, enjoy your many passions without feeling overwhelmed. By combining these elements, you can create your unique life blueprint.

Explore – Manifest – Prioritise – Organise – Weave – Empower - Reflect.

I AM
A VIBRANT
BLEND OF
DIVERSE
PASSIONS
AND TALENTS

Chapter 2

Exploring systems for busy minds

Until recently, I had never heard the term "multi-passionate," I had no idea that several systems describe people like me.

Discovering these systems was one of my most liberating realisations: I don't need to confine myself to just one passion or career. Embracing multiple interests has brought me immense joy and a deep sense of fulfilment.

Over the years, thinkers and creatives have developed different systems and methods to describe and support individuals like us to help make sense of our thoughts.

Let's explore some systems developed for multi-passionate people. Take Multipotentiality, for example. I've always been deeply interested in learning different subjects, even if they didn't connect. In school, I'd be just as fascinated by biology, geography, and history as cooking, science and sewing, anything where I could showcase my creativity. This endless curiosity has stayed with me throughout my life.

Then there's the Renaissance Soul. (Lobenstine, 2006) This one hit home. I have a strong desire for variety and am passionate about lifelong learning. Over the past 30 years, I've continuously engaged in some form of study or another, always eager to learn something new. From pottery to crystals, I've dipped my toes in countless pools of knowledge.

The Scanner Personality (Sher, 1994) also resonates with me. I'm naturally curious and creative and get a real thrill from starting new projects. I crave the excitement of new beginnings, although this often means many projects must be completed. My studio is a testament to this, filled with half-completed projects and half-read books.

The Neo-Generalist (Mikkelsen, 2016) describes my work life perfectly. I've had various career experiences, including retail, admin, design, and banking. I've enjoyed the challenge of learning new skills and adapting to different environments.

Finally, the concept of a slash career (Alboher, 2007) made me smile. My bio tagline proudly reads Author/Artist/Creative. This term acknowledges the multiple roles I happily juggle professionally.

Discovering these systems has been like finding the missing pieces to a puzzle. Knowing that my diverse interests and varied career paths are valid and celebrated is comforting and empowering.

Each of these systems provides a unique perspective on being multi-passionate. They offer validation and practical advice for living a fulfilling life that honours your diverse interests.

After researching these various systems, I identified with many aspects of each, yet I needed clarification. Each system offered valuable insights, but trying to apply all of them at once left me feeling overwhelmed. That's when I realised I needed a simplified approach that worked for me.

I wanted to embrace the concept that having multiple passions or jobs was acceptable and develop an actionable, flexible, and easy-to-follow framework. This led me to create the EMPOWER method: a practical, step-by-step guide that helps multi-passionate individuals like myself turn their diverse interests into their greatest strengths without confusion or complexity.

In the next chapter, I'm excited to introduce you to the EMPOWER method, a framework designed to help multi-passionate individuals like you manage your various interests and transform them into a cohesive, fulfilling life. It simplifies balancing wellness, creativity, and passion while giving you the tools to feel empowered in your unique journey.

Get ready to discover how EMPOWER can help you organise your passions, prioritise what truly matters, and embrace the freedom to live a vibrant, multi-dimensional life. The world needs your unique contributions and the richness you bring by being true to yourself.

I AM
CAPABLE OF
EXPLORING
MANY INTERESTS
AND EXCELLING
IN ALL

SECTION 2

Introducing the EMPOWER Method

Chapter 3

Empower Yourself

Now that we've explored the journey that led me to develop my system for thriving as a multi-passionate person, it's time to dive into the core of this book: The EMPOWER Method.

This method was developed from my personal experiences. It blends strategies from different techniques and is fine-tuned into a process that works for those juggling multiple interests and resonates with more than one system.

It's designed to help you organise, prioritise, and, most importantly, enjoy your many passions without feeling overwhelmed or guilty. Get ready to embrace your multi-passionate self in a way that feels freeing, fulfilling, and aligned with the life you've always wanted to live.

Imagine waking up daily with peace and purpose, no longer burdened by the pressure to "choose one thing" or conform to a narrow mould. You feel aligned with yourself, embracing all your passions without guilt or overwhelm. You're no longer wrestling with indecision or feeling stuck; instead, you live a life that reflects the full spectrum of who you are—a person thriving in every aspect.

A life where you can explore various interests without feeling like you have to sacrifice one for another. You crave the freedom to pursue everything that inspires you while staying grounded and focused. You aim to be the best version of yourself—someone confident, fulfilled, and in control of their time and energy. Other people's expectations no longer define you. You define yourself by what brings you joy, creativity, and growth.

Life isn't about perfection. It's not about forcing yourself to settle on one passion or path. Instead, it's about the freedom to explore, create, and express yourself fully. With the EMPOWER method, you'll realise that your diverse interests are your superpower, not something to hide or downplay.

You'll feel liberated to express yourself through multiple activities, knowing that each adds richness and meaning to your life. Imagine feeling confident in your choices, no longer second-guessing yourself or wondering if you should "just focus on one thing." You've learned how to prioritise in the moment, and you trust that all of your passions have their time and place. You're flourishing, not despite your multi-passionate nature but because of it.

The EMPOWER method helps you embrace this multiplicity without stress or guilt. You don't have to feel bad for wanting to do it all. Instead, you'll feel good about it. You'll understand how to manage your energy and your time so that every part of you gets to shine. You're no longer trying to fit into someone else's definition of success. Instead, you're creating your own, filled with passion, purpose, and creative fire.

EMPOWER System

Explore: Identify and explore all your interests and passions.

Manifest: Envision how your diverse passions can coexist in a balanced, fulfilling life.

Prioritise: Choose which passion to focus on in the moment.

Organise: Create a flexible system to balance your many interests.

Weave: Find ways to integrate your passions so they work together.

Empower: Embrace your multi-passionate identity with confidence.

Reflect: Regularly review and adjust your focus to align with your evolving passions.

I AM CONFIDENT IN MY ABILITY TO BALANCE MULTIPLE PASSIONS

Chapter 4

E. EXPLORE

Discover the full range of your passions. In this step, you allow yourself to thoroughly explore all your interests without judgment or the need to "pick one." Exploration is about curiosity, self-discovery, and embracing the idea that having multiple passions is okay. You'll start by identifying the things that excite you—creative pursuits, hobbies, or potential career paths—and permit yourself to explore them without the pressure to master them all.

How to explore: List all your passions, from minor curiosities to lifelong interests. Be open to trying new things and deepening existing interests.

Outcome: You gain clarity on the scope of your passions and begin to see them as a source of possibility, not a burden or confusion.

Identify and Explore All Your Interests and Passions

Imagine standing at the edge of a forest, knowing it's full of hidden paths, fascinating creatures, and untold discoveries. The air is alive with possibility. You've been told to pick one path and stick with it, but deep down, you feel pulled in many directions—because why limit yourself to just one adventure? This forest represents your passions, interests, and curiosities. The question isn't which path you should take but how to embrace its richness.

In this chapter, we'll begin your journey into exploration. This is the first and most crucial step in the EMPOWER System because it sets the foundation for everything that follows. Here, you'll learn how to identify your passions, understand their value, and permit yourself to explore them fully—without judgment or fear. Remember, your curiosity isn't a burden; it's a gift that leads to more profound self-discovery and a more fulfilled life.

Why should we allow ourselves to explore?

For multi-passionate women, the pressure to focus on a single passion or career path can suffocate. Society tends to celebrate specialists—those who've seemingly found their "one thing" and mastered it. But if you're someone who lights up at the thought of many different interests, this can make you feel lost or inadequate. Exploring multiple passions allows you to live a more vibrant, creative, and well-rounded life.

When you explore your passions, you discover what truly excites you. Some passions may become long-term companions, while others might serve a shorter purpose, offering joy or learning before they fade. The beauty of exploration is that it's not about choosing but learning. The more you explore, the more insight you gain about yourself and how your passions fit into your unique journey.

Step 1: Permit Yourself to Be Curious

The first step in exploring your passions is permitting yourself. Society has conditioned many of us to feel that we must pick a lane, commit to it, and never look back. This chapter is about unlearning that narrative. You don't need to justify your interests to anyone, including yourself. You have the right to be curious and the freedom to pursue as many passions as you desire.

Action Step:

Journal Prompt: List all the interests, hobbies, or passions that light you up. Don't censor yourself—whether it's knitting, learning a new language, starting a podcast, or gardening, everything counts. This is your opportunity to honour all parts of yourself.

Reminder:

It's okay if some interests seem fleeting or don't fit into your current life. You're not deciding which ones to pursue right now; you're simply exploring what excites you.

Step 2: Let Go of the Pressure to Choose

A vital part of the exploration process is letting go of the pressure to choose just one thing. Your life is a complex path that weaves in many directions to reach its final destination. Think of it as a patchwork quilt, where each passion or interest forms a unique part of the whole. You're not abandoning any path; instead, you're weaving them together.

The notion that we must choose a single passion originates from a limited perspective on success and fulfilment. Multi-passionate individuals like you often excel when they allow themselves to explore various paths. Many remarkable innovators, creators, and leaders have been multi-passionate, weaving their interests into something extraordinary.

Action Step:

Reflection Exercise: Think back to when you were a child. What activities, hobbies, or interests excited you before the pressure of "finding your path" set in? Often, our childhood passions hold clues to the things we still love but may have been conditioned to ignore.

Step 3: Dive Deep into Each Passion

Now that you've identified your interests, it's time to dive deeper into them. Exploring a passion doesn't mean you need to become an expert immediately—it's about immersing yourself in the experience and seeing where it takes you. Some passions may pull you in immediately, while others might require more time to reveal their value. The key is to immerse yourself fully without worrying about where it will lead.

You might discover new layers of your interests that you never considered before. For example, if you love writing, explore different genres—fiction, poetry, personal essays, and journaling. If you're passionate about cooking, experiment with various cuisines or try your hand at food photography. Exploration is about giving yourself the freedom to play.

Action Step:

Experiment: Choose one of your passions and dedicate the next week to exploring it. Set aside a specific time each day, even if it's just 30 minutes. Immerse yourself in that passion without any pressure to achieve mastery.

Step 4: Embrace Exploration as an Ongoing Process

One of the biggest misconceptions about exploring passions is that it's a one-time event. In reality, exploration is a lifelong process. As we grow and evolve, so do our interests and passions. Some passions may fade while others emerge. The important thing is to continue giving yourself permission to explore and re-explore. What excites you today might not be what excites you a year from now—and that's perfectly okay.

Embrace exploration as a way of staying connected to yourself. Your passions reflect your inner world, and continuing to explore them aligns you with your ever-evolving identity.

True fulfilment lies not in finding a singular passion but in allowing yourself to explore the fullness of your curiosity.

Action Step:

Monthly Check-In: At the end of each month, take a moment to reflect on which passions or interests are currently energising you. Have any new ones emerged? Are there ones you wish to explore further? Use this opportunity to remain open and curious about your evolving interests.

The Power of Exploration

Exploration is the gateway to self-discovery and fulfilment. When you embrace your multi-passionate nature and permit yourself to explore, you broaden your understanding of the world and yourself. This chapter signifies the beginning of your journey towards embracing your passions, and it starts with the permission to explore.

You don't have to fit into a one-size-fits-all box and certainly don't have to choose one path over another. By exploring your interests, you're giving yourself the freedom to lead a rich, fulfilling life that honours every part of you.

I AM
UNIQUE
AND MY
MULTI-
PASSIONATE
NATURE IS
MY
STRENGTH

Chapter 5

M. MANIFEST

Envision a life where all your passions thrive.
This step involves manifesting a vision where your passions harmonise with your life. You don't have to "choose one thing," but you need to create a vision of how your passions can coexist in an aligned way. This is where you start imagining what balance looks like and how you want to incorporate your passions into your daily life.

How to manifest: Visualise the ideal life that allows room for your passions. Create a vision board, write down your dream day, and focus on how your passions can enrich your life.

Outcome: You have a clear vision for the life you want to live—one where all your passions have space to flourish. This will serve as your North Star as you move through the rest of the system.

Now that you've permitted yourself to explore your passions, the next step is manifesting a life where these passions coexist harmoniously. Instead of trying to force your interests into separate, disconnected boxes, imagine weaving them together into a life that feels balanced, fulfilling, and uniquely yours. Manifesting is about creating a vision for your life—a roadmap that guides you from exploration to integration.

This chapter will explore how to embrace your diverse passions and visualise a future where they can flourish together. It's not about overwhelming yourself with too many commitments; it's about crafting a life where your passions enhance each other and contribute to a sense of balance. This is where you transform the energy of exploration into a joyful, actionable vision for your multi-passionate life.

Why Should We Manifest?

For many multi-passionate people, the challenge isn't having interests but believing that it's possible to live a life where all those interests can coexist peacefully. You might have been told that too many passions lead to chaos, overwhelm, or lack of focus. But when you consciously manifest a vision for your life, you take control of how your passions will work together rather than letting them pull you in different directions.

Manifesting is creating a clear mental picture of your ideal life. It's about imagining a future where your passions are integrated, balanced, and fulfilling—where you're not forced to choose between them; instead, they all have their place. This step is critical to transforming your passions from scattered interests into a harmonious, purposeful life.

Step 1: Clarify Your Vision

The first step to manifesting a life that embraces your diverse passions is to get clear on your vision. Ask yourself: What would my ideal day, week, or month look like if all my passions had a place? Visualise how your various interests can fit together into a cohesive lifestyle. This isn't about overloading yourself but understanding where each passion fits into the bigger picture.

Action Step:

Visualisation Exercise: Close your eyes and imagine a day in your ideal life. How are you incorporating your different passions? What activities fill your day? How do you feel when all of your interests are being fulfilled in a balanced way? Write down what you see, focusing on the balance and how each passion fits into your life.

Reminder: Manifesting your vision isn't about perfection. It's about giving yourself a clear direction. Your vision will evolve, but having this roadmap helps you stay grounded and intentional as you move forward.

Step 2: Create a Life of Synergy

One of the most powerful aspects of manifesting is realising that your passions don't need to be separated or compartmentalised. Rather than viewing each interest as a distinct, isolated activity, consider how they can enhance one another. Creating synergy is a dynamic in which your passions interact and support each other.

For example, if you're passionate about photography and wellness, how can you combine these passions? Could you take nature photography during your outdoor adventures? Could you merge your love for writing with your passion for creative expression by starting a blog about your journey? When you manifest a life of synergy, your passions begin to feel interconnected, creating a fluid and natural lifestyle.

Action Step:

Synergy Mapping: Draw a circle in the centre of your page and write "My Passions." Around the circle, note down each of your passions. Then, draw lines between them where you identify potential overlaps or areas of synergy. Look for places where your interests might naturally connect, support, or inspire one another.

Outcome:

By identifying these areas of synergy, you'll begin to see how your passions can collaborate instead of competing for your attention. This shift in mindset allows you to visualise a life where all your interests flourish together.

Step 3: Set Intentions for Each Passion

Once you've visualised how your passions can coexist and identified areas of synergy, it's time to set intentions. Intentions differ from goals in that they're not about achieving a specific outcome but about focusing your energy and attention in a way that aligns with your vision. Setting intentions for each passion helps you stay grounded and ensures that you're nurturing all of your interests in a manageable way.

For example, your intention for creative expression might be to paint once a week to relax and recharge, while your intention for wellness might be to dedicate time each morning to yoga or meditation. By setting intentions, you avoid overwhelm and ensure you give space to each passion without stretching yourself too thin.

Action Step:

Intention Setting: Write a clear intention for each passion you identified in the previous chapter. Keep it simple and focused on how you want that passion to enrich your life.

"I intend to cultivate my passion for photography by exploring nature and capturing beauty every weekend."

"I intend to nurture my love of writing by journaling for 15 minutes each morning or on Wednesdays and Fridays."

Outcome:

These intentions will act as anchors, helping you integrate your passions into your daily life purposefully and sustainably.

Step 4: Design a Balanced Lifestyle

Manifesting a life where your passions coexist isn't just about thinking and visualising—it's about designing a lifestyle that supports balance. This means taking practical steps to ensure you have the time, energy, and space for your passions. Balance doesn't mean dividing your time equally among your interests, but rather, creating a flow that allows you to engage with each passion as it fits into your life.

Consider how your passions integrate into your broader lifestyle, which encompasses work, relationships, and self-care. If a particular passion demands more of your time during specific periods (such as a project or career emphasis), you may want to temporarily reduce your focus on others. The objective is to adapt, maintain a balanced flow, and align with your current priorities.

Action Step:

Create a Passion Calendar: Review your week or month and set aside specific times for each passion. To avoid overwhelming yourself, begin with small, realistic time blocks that feel manageable. For instance, you could plan for creative expression on Saturdays, morning wellness, and community connection on Wednesday evenings.

Outcome:

By designing a flexible but intentional lifestyle, you give yourself the space to honour your passions without feeling pulled in too many directions.

Step 5: Trust the Process

Manifesting a balanced, fulfilling life with your diverse passions is ongoing. As you grow, your interests will evolve, and your vision will shift. Trusting that your passions lead you toward an authentic and aligned life is vital. It's also essential to remain flexible and open to changes.

Manifesting doesn't mean everything will happen overnight. Instead, it's about taking consistent, aligned action toward your vision, trusting that your envisioned life will unfold over time. This book took two years from manifesting to completion!

Action Step:

Daily Manifestation Practice: Each day, dedicate a few minutes to visualising your ideal life, where all your passions harmoniously coexist. Focus on how it feels, the joy it brings, and how balanced it appears. This daily practice keeps your vision clear and reminds you of the life you are actively creating.

Outcome:

By trusting the process and regularly revisiting your vision, you remain aligned with your purpose, constantly refining and adjusting to stay balanced.

The Power of Manifestation

Manifestation is a powerful tool for transforming your multi-passionate nature into a balanced and fulfilling life. By visualising how your passions can coexist, creating synergy, setting clear intentions, and designing a lifestyle that supports balance, you're actively crafting a life that honours all parts of yourself.

Remember, manifesting isn't about trying to do everything at once—it's about allowing your passions to flow naturally, giving each one time and space. As you move forward, trust that the life you've envisioned is within reach, and let your passions guide you toward the balance and fulfilment you deserve.

I AM
OPEN
TO THE
POSSIBILITIES
MY DIVERSE
INTERESTS
CREATE

Chapter 6

P. PRIORITISE

Identify and focus on what's most important at the moment. Multi-passionate individuals often feel overwhelmed by the sheer number of their interests, which leads to scattered energy and frustration. The Prioritise step helps you recognise which passion or project needs attention at any given time. It's not about abandoning other interests; it's about understanding where to focus your energy right now.

How to prioritise: Take into account factors such as your current life goals, your available energy, deadlines, and which passion is most compelling to you.

Outcome: You feel less scattered and clearer-headed, knowing you're dedicating your time to something meaningful without neglecting your other passions—they'll have their moment.

Choose Which Passion to Focus on in the Moment

Now that you've explored your passions and visualised a vision where they can all coexist, it's time to take the next step: prioritise. If you're multi-passionate, you likely love many things at once, making it hard to decide where to focus your attention. The good news is that prioritising doesn't mean abandoning your other interests—it simply means choosing where to direct your energy at the moment. Think of it as determining what deserves your attention in this season of life, knowing that you can return to other passions when the time is right.

In this chapter, we will identify the passion or project that requires immediate attention without making you neglect your other interests. Prioritising is about gaining clarity, alleviating overwhelm, and ensuring your efforts are intentional and aligned with your goals.

Why should we prioritise this?

One of the biggest challenges for multi-passionate women is feeling torn between their various interests. With so many things pulling at your heart, it's easy to become overwhelmed. However, attempting to do everything at once often leads to burnout and frustration. The solution isn't to restrict yourself to one thing permanently but to concentrate on what matters most now.

Prioritising enables you to channel your energy effectively. It helps you take decisive action on one passion or project while allowing you to explore your other interests later. Instead of being stuck in analysis paralysis or trying to juggle too much, prioritising allows you to progress in a focused and intentional manner.

Step 1: Identify Your Current Life Goals

The first step to prioritising is to clarify your current life goals. These are the more significant objectives that shape what's important to you now. Your goals may change over time, but they are a compass for deciding which passion or project to focus on. What do you want to accomplish in the next few months or years? Is your focus on personal growth, career development, financial stability, or creative expression?

For instance, during a crucial season for advancing your career, you should focus on passions or projects that support your professional growth. If you are more reflective or creative, you should emphasise pursuits that allow you to express yourself, such as writing, painting, or personal projects.

Action Step:

Goal Clarity Exercise: Write down your top 3-5 life goals for the next 6-12 months. Be specific and focus on what's most important to you right now. These goals will help guide which passions deserve your attention.

Outcome:

By clarifying your goals, you create a framework for prioritising. This gives you a clearer picture of which passion aligns with your current direction.

Step 2: Evaluate the Joy Each Passion Brings

Once you've clarified your life goals, it's time to evaluate the energy and joy that each of your passions brings. Some interests will naturally energise and excite you, while others may feel draining or burdensome, especially if tied to external pressures or expectations. It's crucial to focus on the passions that inspire you and provide energy because those are the ones that will propel you forward without leaving you burnt out.

Ask yourself:

Which passions are currently bringing me the most joy? Which ones feel aligned with my energy at the moment? Sometimes, a passion you've cherished in the past may not feel as exciting right now, and that's perfectly fine. You can prioritise the right passions for this season by assessing your energy levels.

Action Step:

Energy Check: Rate each passion on your list on a scale of 1-10 based on how much energy and joy it brings you. Pay attention to the ones that score highest—they're likely the ones that deserve your focus.

Outcome:

You'll understand which passions are currently energising you and which might need to be put on hold. This will help you decide what will fuel your well-being and creativity.

Step 3: Assess Time and Resources

Prioritising also requires a realistic assessment of your time and resources. While some passions may excite you, they might not be feasible right now due to time constraints, financial limitations, or other responsibilities. For instance, if you're passionate about travelling but can't take time off work, this may not be the ideal moment to focus on that passion.

This step is about looking at your current capacity. Consider how much time you can realistically dedicate to each passion. Some passions require more time or financial investment, so assessing what's feasible right now is vital. This doesn't mean you're saying no forever—it just means you're pacing yourself.

Action Step:

Time and Resource Audit: List your top passions and evaluate the time, money, and resources each requires. Consider your current schedule and commitments, and based on your availability, identify which passions are most realistic to prioritise.

Outcome:

You'll clearly understand which passions fit into your current life, ensuring you can focus without spreading yourself too thin or taking on more than you can handle.

Step 4: Make Peace with Temporary Trade-Offs

One of the most complex parts of prioritising is making peace with temporary trade-offs. Being multi-passionate often means feeling like you're "missing out" on something when you focus on one passion over another. However, it's important to remember that prioritising doesn't mean giving up on your other interests—it simply means they'll have their moment when the time is right.

Trade-offs are temporary. By choosing one passion to focus on now, you're creating space for others to flourish in the future. This shift in mindset can help you feel less guilty about putting specific passions on hold and more excited about the ones you prioritise.

Action Step:

Mindset Shift Exercise: Write down the passion you choose to focus on and list the benefits of prioritising it right now. Then, note the passions you're temporarily setting aside and remind yourself that they aren't disappearing—they're just waiting for their chance.

Outcome:

You'll feel a sense of peace knowing that you're making an intentional choice rather than feeling like you're abandoning any of your passions. This will help you focus entirely on what's in front of you.

Step 5: Set Clear, Focused Goals for Your Passion

Now that you've decided which passion to prioritise, it's time to set clear, focused goals. This step helps you move from intention to action. Setting specific, actionable goals ensures that you're making progress meaningfully and helps keep you accountable to your chosen passion.

Your goals should align with your life vision and feel attainable within your set timeframe. Begin with small, achievable steps that create momentum. For example, if you've chosen to prioritise your passion for creative writing, a potential goal could be to write for 30 minutes each morning or to complete one short story by the end of the month.

Action Step:

Goal-Setting: For the passion you've prioritised, set 1-3 clear goals for the next month. Be specific about what you want to achieve and how you'll measure your progress. Make sure these goals feel aligned with your energy and current life circumstances.

Outcome:

With clear goals, you'll have a roadmap for making tangible progress in your chosen passion. This keeps you focused and motivated as you move forward.

The Power of Prioritising

Prioritising is a skill that allows you to make intentional decisions about where to focus your energy without sacrificing your multi-passionate nature. By clarifying your current goals, assessing your energy and resources, and making peace with temporary trade-offs, you can confidently choose the passion that deserves your attention. This approach helps you feel more grounded, focused, and capable of progressing, even when many interests are vying for your time.

Remember, prioritising doesn't mean abandoning your other passions—it simply means focusing on one right now, knowing that the others will have their time. By channelling your energy into what's most important at the moment, you're building a life that honours all your passions in a sustainable, fulfilling way.

I AM
RESILIENT
AND
ADAPTABLE
AND CAN
THRIVE IN
ALL MY
ENDEAVOURS

Chapter 7

O. ORGANISE

After prioritising, the next step is to create a structure that keeps you organised without feeling restrictive. Organising involves designing a system or schedule that allows you to pursue multiple passions in a manageable way. It's not about rigid time blocking; instead, it's about giving each passion its own space and avoiding the sensation of chaos.

How to organise: Use tools like flexible schedules, task batching, or project planning. Break down your passions into smaller, achievable actions that fit into your daily or weekly routine.

Outcome: You have a plan that accommodates all your passions without trying to juggle everything simultaneously. This reduces stress and gives you the freedom to explore each interest.

A Flexible Structure That Accommodates Multiple Passions

Now that you've learned to prioritise one passion at a time, it's time to bring order and flow into your multi-passionate life. Organising doesn't mean rigid schedules or trying to do everything at once; instead, it's about creating a flexible structure that allows your passions to coexist harmoniously. Structure doesn't limit creativity—in fact, it frees you from the chaos of feeling scattered by providing a straightforward way to manage your passions in a balanced, sustainable manner.

In this chapter, we'll explore how to organise your time, energy, and resources in a way that works for you. Your life isn't a cookie-cutter version of anyone else's or your structure. You'll learn to create a personalised, flexible framework that lets you thrive in your passions without feeling overwhelmed or boxed in.

Why Flexible Structure Matters

As a multi-passionate person, you've likely felt the tug-of-war between your interests. Without a structure, it can seem like you're perpetually chasing different passions, uncertain how to balance them all. Rigid schedules may leave you feeling trapped, especially if your creativity ebbs and flows. This is where a flexible structure proves beneficial—it enables you to honour all your passions while allowing space for spontaneity and creative exploration.

A flexible structure provides the balance between having direction and allowing freedom. It helps you avoid burnout, manage your time wisely, and create a rhythm that suits your unique lifestyle. By the end of this chapter, you'll have the tools to build a structure that supports your multi-passionate nature while giving each passion the attention it deserves.

Step 1: Time Block with Flexibility

One of the most effective ways to create a flexible structure is through time blocking, dedicating specific time blocks to certain activities or passions. Unlike a rigid schedule, time blocking allows you to focus on one task at a time while being adaptable enough to manage unexpected events. This method helps you maintain balance without feeling overwhelmed.

The key to successful time blocking is to remain flexible. Adjust your blocks if something doesn't go as planned or a passion requires more time than anticipated. Think of time blocking as a guide, not a rulebook.

Action Step:

Create Your Time Blocks: Review your week and set specific time slots for each passion. You might dedicate mornings to writing, afternoons to wellness practices, and weekends to your creative hobbies. Leave blank space for relaxation or unstructured time to explore whichever passion feels most vibrant.

Outcome:

You'll have a clear visual map of your week that gives you time to focus on each passion without feeling overwhelmed. This structure keeps you productive while allowing flexibility when needed.

Step 2: Use the "Theme Day" Approach

If juggling multiple passions feels overwhelming, consider assigning theme days to your week. This method works exceptionally well if you have several unrelated passions requiring different energy types. For example, you might dedicate Mondays to creative work, Tuesdays to personal development, and Wednesdays to wellness practices. This approach allows you to focus on one area at a time, preventing the need to switch gears constantly.

Theme days prevent you from feeling scattered because they allow you to immerse yourself fully in one passion without guilt. They also help you batch your tasks and passions to make your time more efficient.

Action Step:

Plan Your Theme Days: Reflect on your passions and think about grouping similar interests. If you're juggling a job with your creative pursuits, consider setting aside certain days to focus on your passions outside of work hours. For instance, I dedicate Mondays to writing, Wednesdays to wellness, and Fridays to creative exploration. Adjust the days to fit your schedule, but maintain these days for consistency.

Outcome:

Your week will have a sense of rhythm and structure, which helps prevent burnout and gives each project its dedicated time. This creates a natural flow, allowing you to immerse yourself in one project at a time without feeling guilty about others.

Step 3: The Power of Small, Consistent Actions

When you have multiple projects or passions, it's easy to feel you need long periods to dedicate to each one. However, small, consistent actions can lead to significant progress without overwhelming your schedule. Even if you only have 15 to 30 minutes daily, consistently working on your projects accumulates over time.

Rather than waiting for the perfect moment or large blocks of time, commit to taking small steps each day toward your passions. Whether writing a few pages, practising a skill, or doing something creative, these small actions keep your passions alive and thriving.

Action Step:

Set Daily Mini-Goals: For each project, establish a small, actionable goal you can achieve in 15 to 30 minutes. For instance, if one of your passions is painting, commit to sketching for 20 minutes each morning. If another passion is learning a new language, dedicate 15 minutes to practising every evening. These mini-goals easily fit into your day and help you progress.

Outcome:

You'll build momentum in your projects without feeling overwhelmed by the need for perfection or significant time commitments. Small, consistent actions lead to long-term success and fulfilment.

Step 4: Rest and Unstructured Time

Being multi-passionate often means bursting with energy and ideas, but it's crucial to remember that rest and unstructured time are just as valuable as action. Over-scheduling yourself can lead to burnout, even when you're engaged in activities you love. Setting aside time for relaxation, reflection, and spontaneous creativity is essential.

Unstructured time allows you to explore whichever passion excites you most. It also gives your mind and body time to recharge, making it easier to return to structured activities with renewed energy. Rest is essential for maintaining the balance between structure and freedom.

Action Step:

Schedule Rest Periods: Each week, block out time when you do nothing related to productivity. This might look like walking in nature, reading for pleasure, or simply relaxing with no agenda. Make sure this time is genuinely unstructured—no "guilt" attached to not being productive.

Outcome:

Building rest into your routine prevents burnout and maintains your energy for your passions. Unstructured time also allows for spontaneous bursts of creativity, which can lead to new ideas and insights.

Step 5: Use Tools to Stay Organized

Staying organised doesn't have to be complicated. Many tools help you track your passions, projects, and time. Whether you prefer digital tools or physical planners, finding a system that works for you is vital to maintaining balance. Tools like calendars, task managers, and project boards can help you stay focused and organised, ensuring you're making progress without feeling overwhelmed.

Here are some tools to consider:

Calendars: Use a digital or physical calendar to allocate time for your interests, deadlines, and free time.

Task Managers: Tools like *Trello, Asana, Monday.com* or *Todoist* or something similar can help you manage projects related to each passion. I used Trello for collaborations with my first books. Most of these task managers have a free version so you can try them out first. experiment and see which ones work for you.

Journals or Planners: A daily planner or bullet journal can help you stay grounded in your weekly goals and tasks.

Action Step:

Choose Your Tools: Select a tool or system that suits your style—a digital calendar, task management app, or physical planner. Use it to track each passion's time blocks, theme days, and mini-goals. Keep things simple and steer clear of complicating your system unnecessarily.

Outcome:

With the right tools, you'll feel more in control of your schedule and passions. This will reduce your feelings of being overwhelmed and provide you with a clear roadmap for each day, week, and month.

By utilising time blocks, theme days, and small, consistent actions, you establish a structure that aligns with your life rather than contradicting it. You're not forcing yourself to pick between your passions and projects—instead, you're allowing each one time and space.

I AM
AN INSPIRING
EXAMPLE OF
A LIFE LIVED
WITH CURIOSITY
AND CREATIVITY

Chapter 8

W. WEAVE

Integrate your passions into a harmonious whole. The Weave step is about finding creative ways to connect your passions and projects to complement each other. You look for synergy rather than treat each interest as a separate entity. Can one passion inspire another? Can they intersect in a way that amplifies both? Weaving your passions together creates a sense of cohesion and reduces the internal tension that comes from feeling like you have to choose between them.

How to weave: Look for overlap between your interests. For example, can you combine your love of photography with your interest in wellness by documenting outdoor retreats? Can your passion for writing fuel your interest in creative expression or business?

Outcome: Your projects feel interconnected, and you no longer see them as competing forces. This creates a sense of fulfilment because you live more holistically.

Integrate Your Passions So They Complement Each Other

You've learned how to prioritise and organise your projects within a flexible structure, but now it's time to unite them in a cohesive and connected way. Rather than treating each project as a separate, isolated entity, the key to thriving as a multi-passionate person lies in weaving your projects and passions together. This approach allows your interests to complement and enrich, creating synergy instead of conflict or competition.

This chapter will explore integrating your passions and projects to enhance your life experience. Weaving your passions together doesn't mean forcing them into one category; instead, it's about finding creative ways to interact. When you achieve this, your passions become part of a unified whole, contributing to a fluid, purposeful, and aligned life.

Why should we weave our projects and passions together?

As a multi-passionate person, you may sometimes feel like you're living in different worlds, with each of your interests pulling you in various directions. This can result in fragmentation, where you leap from one passion to another without a clear connection. Weaving addresses this by allowing your passions to enhance one another. Rather than viewing them as separate, you can see how they can collaborate to create a more prosperous and fulfilling life.

Weaving your passions involves discovering where your interests overlap and connecting meaningfully. When you weave, you no longer feel pressured to categorise your passions. Instead, you cultivate a lifestyle that naturally transitions from one interest to another, seamlessly integrating your passions into a unified, purpose-driven life.

Step 1: Identify Areas of Synergy (revisit your previous notes)

The first step in weaving your passions is to identify areas of synergy—we did an action activity in the manifesting chapter. We will work on this again here.

For instance, if you're passionate about science and art, can you combine these interests by creating artwork or jewellery inspired by close up photographs of the eyeball? The key is to seek opportunities where your passions can coexist and enhance one another.

Action Step: (redo this activity again)

Synergy Mapping: Draw a diagram with each of your passions as a circle. Start by drawing lines between any passions that naturally overlap. Write down potential projects or ideas that could bring these passions together. For example, if you love design and entrepreneurship, you could explore creating a personal brand around design services.

Outcome:

You'll discover how your passions can connect and support one another. This mapping exercise will help you uncover new opportunities for integration, enabling your passions to flow together more seamlessly.

Step 2: Build Projects that Bridge Passions

Once you've identified areas of synergy, the next step is to create projects that connect your passions. Instead of viewing each passion as a separate entity, consider projects or activities that meld multiple interests into one cohesive endeavour. This approach enables you to express more than one passion simultaneously without the feeling of dividing your energy.

For example, if you're enthusiastic about wellness and creative writing, you might write a book or start a blog that explores the relationship between self-care and creativity. If you're passionate about fitness and photography, think about setting up a fitness-focused Instagram account to showcase your workouts and visual content. Focusing on projects that connect your passions will help you feel more fulfilled as you engage with various aspects of yourself.

Action Step:

Create a Bridge Project: Select two or more passions from your list and brainstorm a project that allows you to engage with both. The project can be big or small—anything from a creative side hustle to a personal blog or a collaborative art project. The aim is to create something that reflects more than one of your interests.

Outcome:

You'll have a tangible project that weaves your passions, giving you a sense of purpose and alignment. This project will help you feel more connected to your passions while reducing the need to categorise your interests.

Step 3: Leverage Transferable Skills

Another powerful way to weave your passions is to leverage transferable skills—the abilities, strengths, and insights you've gained from one passion that can enhance another. For example, if you've developed strong communication skills from your love for public speaking, you can apply those skills to your passion for teaching or coaching. Similarly, if you're skilled in time management, you can use that skill to organise your creative pursuits better.

Recognising that each passion brings valuable skills to enhance your other interests is vital. You create synergy by intentionally applying what you've learned from one area to another and increasing your overall effectiveness. This allows your passions to support each other rather than compete for your attention.

Action Step:

Transferable Skills Audit: List skills you've developed from each of your passions. Then, identify how those skills can be applied to other passions or areas of your life. For example, if you've developed a knack for storytelling through your love of writing, think about how that skill can enhance your passion for speaking or teaching.

Outcome:

Recognising and using transferable skills will strengthen your passions and create a more cohesive sense of self. This will help you see how each passion adds value to the others, making integrating them into your life easier.

Step 4: Collaborate and Connect with Like-Minded People

Weaving your passions doesn't always have to be a solo endeavour. Sometimes, the best way to integrate your interests is to collaborate with others who share similar passions or connect with like-minded communities. Collaborations allow you to engage with multiple passions while leveraging the strengths of others. They also open up new opportunities to grow and explore in ways you might not have considered.

For example, if you're passionate about art and wellness, you could collaborate with a wellness coach to create a visual art project focused on mental health. If you love music and social causes, you might collaborate with other musicians to host a benefit concert. Collaboration enriches your passions and brings fresh perspectives that enhance the weaving process.

Action Step:

Consider a Collaboration Opportunity: Think about one of your passions and how you might work with someone with a similar interest. Reach out to that person or community to explore potential projects or partnerships. This could be as simple as hosting a workshop, creating content together, or initiating a joint project.

Outcome:

By collaborating with others, you'll broaden the scope of your passions and find new ways to weave them into your life. You'll also cultivate relationships and connections that enrich your experience and unlock new opportunities for future projects.

Step 5: Embrace the Flow Between Passions

One of the most powerful aspects of weaving is embracing the natural flow between your passions. Instead of trying to balance everything perfectly, weaving allows you to shift your focus among your interests as your energy and priorities change. Some passions may take centre stage for a time, while others recede to the background. The important thing is to let go of the notion that you aren't focused on right now.

Weaving is about flow, not rigid balance. Just as the seasons change, so too will your passions. One month, you may feel more connected to your creative projects; the next, you might dive deeper into your personal development journey. Embrace this flow, knowing that all your passions are part of the same tapestry, even if they take turns coming to the forefront.

Action Step:

Reflect on Your Passion Flow: Examine your current passions and identify which consumes the most energy. Then, consider how this may evolve. Allow yourself to shift your focus as needed, trusting each passion will have time to shine.

Outcome:

Embracing the flow between your passions can reduce the pressure of balancing everything perfectly. It helps you stay aligned with your natural energy, enabling your passions to weave together effortlessly over time.

The Power of Weaving

Weaving your passions together creates a sense of wholeness in your life. By identifying areas of synergy, constructing projects that connect your interests, and embracing the natural flow between your passions, you cultivate a lifestyle where all your interests support and enrich one another. This integration makes you feel more connected to yourself, less fragmented, and more empowered to express your creativity and curiosity.

Remember, weaving is about creating harmony rather than forcing connections. It's about allowing your passions to flow together naturally and recognising that each brings value to the others. By weaving your passions, you cultivate a life that reflects the full spectrum of who you are—creative, curious, and endlessly multi-dimensional.

I AM
FULFILLED
BY THE
RICH
MULTIFACTED
LIFE I
AM LIVING

Chapter 9

E. EMPOWER

Embrace your multi-passionate identity without apology. Multi-passionate people often feel pressured to apologise for their diverse interests or fear being perceived as unfocused. The Empower step is about embracing your multi-passionate nature as a strength. You stop trying to conform to the traditional "one-thing" narrative and start viewing your curiosity and creativity as assets. This shift enables you to confidently pursue multiple passions without guilt or the fear of judgment.

How to empower yourself: Embrace self-acceptance by viewing your multi-passionate nature as a superpower. Surround yourself with supportive people who encourage you to explore your various interests. Learn to say "no" to societal expectations and "yes" to your authentic path.

Outcome: You feel confident and unapologetic about living a multi-passionate life. Instead of shrinking yourself to fit in, you expand and own your journey, knowing that thriving in multiple areas is valid.

Embrace Your Multi-Passionate Identity with Confidence

At this stage in your journey, you've explored your passions, manifested a vision for your life, prioritised what to focus on, organised a flexible structure, and learned how to weave your interests together. It's time to fully step into your power by confidently embracing your multi-passionate identity. This chapter is about owning who you are—without apologies or hesitation—and recognising that your diverse interests are not a weakness or a distraction but a superpower.

In this chapter, we'll explore how to reframe your multi-passionate nature, overcome self-doubt, and embrace a mindset of confidence and empowerment. You'll learn to resist the pressure to "choose one thing" and celebrate your ability to excel in various areas. This chapter is the heart of your transformation, where you fully claim your identity as a multi-passionate person and unlock the freedom to live without limits.

Why Embrace Your Multi-Passionate Identity?

For too long, society has celebrated specialisation and the idea that success comes from mastering and focusing on a single pursuit. If you're multi-passionate, you may have grown up believing that having a variety of interests is a flaw or a sign of being unfocused. However, the truth is that being multi-passionate enables you to live uniquely and powerfully. It allows you to bring a rich diversity of knowledge, creativity, and experience to everything you do. Embracing this identity empowers you and makes you feel proud rather than apologetic about your passions.

When you embrace your multi-passionate identity, you no longer feel the need to fit into a box. You stop hiding or downplaying your interests and begin to see them as integral parts of who you are. This shift in mindset is crucial because it gives you the confidence to pursue multiple passions boldly without worrying about external judgment or internal self-doubt.

Step 1: Reframe the Narrative

The first step to embracing your multi-passionate identity is to reframe the narrative you've been told about having many passions and the idea that success only comes from focusing on one thing. Still, many successful, fulfilled people have achieved greatness by embracing their diverse interests. Think about Leonardo da Vinci, Maya Angelou, or Oprah Winfrey—people who thrived because they followed their curiosity in multiple fields.

Instead of viewing your many passions as a hindrance, see them as a gift. Your ability to explore, learn, and thrive in different areas makes you adaptable, creative, and resilient. You unlock your true potential by embracing the idea that your multi-passionate nature is your superpower.

Action Step:

Flip the Script: Write down any negative beliefs you've internalised about having many passions (e.g., "I'm not focused enough" or "I should just pick one thing"). Then, transform each statement into a positive affirmation celebrating your multi-passionate nature. For instance, *"I'm not focused* *enough"* becomes "*My diverse passions provide me with a unique perspective and enable me to thrive in multiple areas.*"

Outcome:

Reframing the narrative will shift your mindset from seeing your multi-passionate nature as a flaw to recognising it as an incredible strength. This new narrative will empower you to move forward with confidence.

Step 2: Own Your Unique Path

Embracing your multi-passionate identity means taking ownership of your unique path. Your journey won't resemble everyone else's, and that's perfectly fine. You might not travel in a straight line or fit into conventional career moulds, but your path is valid, meaningful, and full of possibilities. Accepting this frees you from the pressure to conform to societal norms or expectations.

Reflect on the passions and experiences that shape your unique journey. Each passion, project, or hobby has played a part in who you are today. Rather than feeling the need to justify or explain your pursuit of multiple interests, celebrate that this enriches your life and makes it diverse. Your journey is a mosaic of experiences only you can create.

Action Step:

Celebrate Your Path: Create a life timeline and highlight the various passions you've pursued. Reflect on how each has contributed to your growth, skills, and happiness. Embrace that your journey is unique and has provided you with a wealth of knowledge and experiences that shape who you are.

Outcome:

By owning your unique path, you'll feel empowered to continue pursuing your passions without fear or apology. This helps you embrace your journey fully, knowing it's leading you exactly where you need to go.

Step 3: Build Unshakable Confidence

Confidence serves as the foundation for fully embracing your multi-passionate identity. To cultivate unshakable confidence, you must believe in your ability to succeed on your terms. Confidence arises from trusting yourself—understanding that you can thrive in various areas, even if your journey diverges from the traditional path.

One way to build confidence is to focus on your wins. Every time you've followed a passion, learned something new or completed a project, you've proven that you can succeed. Start tracking your successes, big and small, and use them as evidence that your multi-passionate nature is a source of strength.

Action Step:

Track Your Wins: Create a "Confidence Journal" where you record all your achievements in your passions and projects—whether it's finishing a creative project, acquiring a new skill, or making strides in a personal interest. Regularly review this journal to remind yourself of your abilities and growth.

Outcome:

Focusing on your successes will build confidence in your ability to pursue multiple passions. This growing confidence will empower you to take on more substantial challenges, follow your curiosity, and live boldly.

Step 4: Stop Seeking Permission

To truly embrace your multi-passionate identity, you must stop seeking permission from others. Whether it's friends, family, colleagues, or society, there's often pressure to follow a more traditional or linear path. However, you are the only person who can decide what's right for you. Seeking external validation or approval can prevent you from fully embracing your passions.

Instead of seeking permission, practice self-validation. Trust your instincts and inner voice. You know what inspires you and aligns with your values and desires. You reclaim your power by allowing yourself to pursue your passions without waiting for anyone else's approval.

Action Step:

Self-Validation Practice: The next time you feel the urge to seek someone's opinion or validation about pursuing a passion, pause and ask yourself, "What do I want?" Write down your answer and commit to following your intuition instead of seeking external approval.

Outcome:

By practising self-validation, you'll feel empowered to confidently pursue your passions, knowing that you don't need permission from anyone but yourself. This encourages you to take ownership of your multi-passionate journey without fearing judgment.

Step 5: Surround Yourself with Support

Confidence is strengthened when you surround yourself with a supportive community that celebrates your multi-passionate nature. Not everyone will understand your desire to pursue multiple interests, and that's okay. What matters is finding the people who encourage you to follow your passions, support your growth, and celebrate your unique path.

Seek out like-minded individuals who are also multi-passionate or appreciate your diverse interests. These people will uplift you, provide valuable insights, and remind you that you're not alone in your journey. Building a supportive network offers you the confidence to pursue your passions without feeling isolated or misunderstood.

Action Step:

Find Your Tribe: Join online communities, local groups, or mastermind circles where multi-passionate individuals gather. These may include creative groups, entrepreneurial communities, or social media groups celebrating diverse interests. Make connections and seek support from those who understand and encourage your journey.

Outcome:

By surrounding yourself with supportive, like-minded individuals, you'll feel more confident in embracing your multi-passionate identity. This community will help reinforce your belief that you can thrive in many areas and live a life that's true to you.

The Power of Embracing Your Multi-Passionate Identity

Fully embracing your multi-passionate identity means living with confidence, freedom, and purpose. When you stop apologising for your diverse interests and start celebrating them as a superpower, you unlock a new level of empowerment. You no longer need to conform to others' expectations or seek validation from others. You're confidently walking your path.

Remember, being multi-passionate is a gift. It means you have a rich life with endless opportunities to explore, create, and grow. You step into a life of limitless potential and fulfilment by embracing who you are and empowering yourself to pursue your passions without fear.

I AM
A COLOURFUL
MIX OF
DIFFERENT
PASSIONS AND
TALENTS

Chapter 10

R. REFLECT

Regularly evaluate your progress and adjust your focus as needed.

The Reflect step is about staying in tune with your journey by regularly checking in with yourself. Being multi-passionate means that your interests will evolve, so it's important to reassess your situation and adjust your focus and structure. Reflection allows you to pivot gracefully, embrace new passions, and refine how you balance them.

How to reflect: Schedule regular check-ins (monthly or quarterly) to review your current priorities and passions. Ask yourself questions like: Are my passions still aligned with my goals? Do I feel fulfilled? Am I balancing my wellness and creativity?

Outcome: You stay aligned with your values and passions, continually refining your journey. This prevents burnout and keeps your life dynamic, ensuring you're constantly growing and exploring in a balanced way.

Regularly Review. Reflect and Adjust Your Focus

As a multi-passionate person, your interests and goals will naturally evolve. You might dive deep into one passion for a few months, only to discover a new interest emerging shortly after. This constant evolution is part of the beauty of being multi-passionate, but it also necessitates regular reflection to ensure you remain aligned with what truly excites you. In this chapter, we'll explore the power of reflection—how to consistently review your passions, assess your progress, and make adjustments that align you with your ever-evolving desires.

Reflection is an ongoing process that helps you stay connected to your passions as they shift and evolve. By incorporating reflection into your routine, you can avoid feeling stuck or overwhelmed and remain flexible enough to embrace new opportunities. This chapter will guide you through a self-assessment process that ensures you live a life in harmony with your passions rather than one driven by external expectations or outdated goals.

Why should we continually reflect?

Life as a multi-passionate person is dynamic—what excites you today might not thrill you a year from now. Because of this, it's essential to carve out regular time for reflection so you can adjust your focus and ensure your passions align with your goals and well-being. Without reflection, you may find yourself caught in old routines or pursuing interests that no longer resonate with you.

Reflection allows you to check in with yourself, recalibrate your goals, and celebrate your progress. It's a moment to pause, reflect on your accomplishments, and look forward to where you want to go. This practice helps you stay aligned with your passions and prevents burnout by ensuring you're pursuing what truly brings you joy rather than feeling obligated to stick with something that no longer fits your vision.

Step 1: Set Regular Reflection Checkpoints

The first step in the reflection process is to set regular checkpoints for reviewing your passions and progress. These checkpoints give you time to assess where you are, what's working, and what might need to change. Reflection isn't a one-time activity—it's an ongoing practice that aligns you with your evolving desires. Depending on your preferences, you might reflect weekly, monthly, or quarterly.

Each reflection checkpoint allows you to pause and ask questions about your passions. Are they still exciting you? Do they still align with your life goals? What progress have you made, and what adjustments do you need to make moving forward?

Action Step:

Choose your reflection schedule: Determine how often you want to evaluate your passions and progress. This could be a weekly Sunday review, a monthly self-check-in, or a quarterly reflection session. Mark these times in your calendar to make them a routine.

Outcome:

By setting regular reflection checkpoints, you'll create space to evaluate your progress and passions, ensuring you stay aligned with your current desires and long-term vision.

Step 2: Celebrate Progress and Wins

Reflection isn't just about adjusting your focus; it's also about celebrating your progress. Taking the time to acknowledge your accomplishments—no matter how big or small—helps build confidence and reinforces the value of your multi-passionate journey. Often, we become so focused on what's next that we forget to celebrate how far we've come.

During your reflection sessions, review your past goals and acknowledge your accomplishments. Whether you've completed a creative project, learned a new skill, or maintained your passions, it's vital to recognise the effort and growth you've achieved.

Action Step:

Make a Win List: At each reflection checkpoint, list wins and accomplishments related to your passions. Be specific about what you've achieved and how it's contributed to your personal or professional growth. For example, you might celebrate finishing a course, launching a new project, or successfully balancing multiple interests.

Outcome:

Celebrating your progress will reinforce your belief in your ability to thrive as a multi-passionate person. This practice boosts your confidence and motivates you to keep moving forward.

Step 3: Evaluate What's Working and What's Not

Reflection is also a time to **evaluate** which passions work for you and which may need adjustment. Sometimes, a passion that once energised you may no longer feel aligned. That's perfectly normal—interests evolve, and your life circumstances change. The key is to be honest about what brings you joy and what might be draining your energy.

During reflection sessions, consider: Which passions still excite and fulfil Me? Which feel more like obligations? Are there any interests I've outgrown? This process helps you identify areas where you need to shift your focus or let go of what no longer serves you.

Action Step:

Passion Audit: Make a list of your current passions and projects and evaluate them. For each one, ask yourself if it's still aligned with your goals and values. Rank them based on how much joy and fulfilment they bring you. If a passion no longer feels exciting, consider whether it's time to let it go or put it on pause.

Outcome:

Regularly evaluating what's working and what's not will ensure that your passions align with your current desires. This approach will help you avoid burnout and focus on what truly matters.

Step 4: Adjust Your Goals and Focus

After evaluating your passions, the next step is adjusting your goals and focusing on your discoveries. Reflection is not just about looking back—it's also about looking forward. As your passions evolve, your goals should evolve, too. If a passion has taken on new meaning or discovered a new interest, adjust your goals to reflect that change.

This is also the time to make practical adjustments to your schedule and priorities. If you've been spreading yourself too thin or focusing too much on one passion at the expense of others, now is the time to recalibrate. Adjusting your focus ensures you always work towards what feels aligned, exciting, and fulfilling.

Action Step:

Set New Goals: Based on your reflection, set 1-3 new goals for the next phase of your multi-passionate journey. These goals should reflect your current priorities and what excites you most. Ensure your goals are specific and actionable, giving you a clear path forward.

Outcome:

Adjusting your goals and focus will align you with your evolving passions. This will ensure your journey is always dynamic and responsive to your current situation.

Step 5: Embrace the Fluidity of Your Journey

The final step in the reflection process is embracing the fluidity of your multi-passionate journey. One of the greatest strengths of being multi-passionate is your ability to adapt and evolve. Your interests and priorities will change, and your path will unfold in ways you can't always predict. Reflection helps you stay flexible and open to these changes.

It's essential to remember that your journey doesn't have to follow a straight path. Just because you're focusing on one project now doesn't mean you can't explore another later. By embracing the fluid nature of your passions, you allow yourself the freedom to grow, change, and pursue whatever excites you at the moment.

Action Step:

Reflect on Your progress and direction:: Take a moment to consider how your passions have evolved. Write down how you have changed, the new interests that have emerged, and how your journey has progressed. Recognise that this fluidity is part of your strength as a multi-passionate individual.

Outcome:

By embracing the fluidity of your journey, you'll feel more at peace with the natural ebb and flow of your passions. This mindset helps you stay open to new opportunities and adjust without guilt or pressure to "stick to one thing."

The Power of Reflection

Reflection is a powerful tool for staying aligned with your evolving passions. By setting regular checkpoints, celebrating your wins, evaluating what works, adjusting your goals, and embracing the fluidity of your journey, you create a dynamic process that supports your growth as a multi-passionate person. Reflection keeps you in tune with yourself and ensures that your passions lead you towards fulfilment and joy.

Remember, reflection isn't just about looking back—it's about staying responsive to where you are now and where you want to go next. As you continue to evolve, this process will help you stay aligned with your true desires and keep you moving forward with clarity and confidence.

In the next chapter, we'll explore what's next—how to take everything you've learned and develop strategies and action steps to continue building a life aligned with your passions and purpose. Take pride in your reflection process, knowing it keeps you connected to your most important passions.

Your journey is uniquely yours, unfolding just as it should.

I AM
NOT DEFINED
BY A SINGLE
PATH
MY DIVERSITY
IS MY
STRENGTH

SECTION 3

Developing Strategies and Actions

Chapter 11

STRATEGIES AND ACTIONS

Section Three will concentrate on transforming your multi-passionate nature into practical, actionable steps that lead you toward the life you aspire to create. It's one thing to recognise your diverse interests, but another to know how to harness them effectively. This section is about developing strategies that work for you—balancing your passions, managing your time, and staying motivated while juggling multiple projects.

By the end of this section, you'll have a toolkit of actionable steps that align with your passions and empower you to thrive in every area of your multi-dimensional life.

Get ready to put your ideas into motion!

Building a Life Aligned with Your Passions and Purpose

You've come a long way in embracing your multi-passionate identity, exploring your interests, weaving them together, and building the confidence to live authentically. You've learned to prioritise what matters most, organise a flexible structure, reflect regularly, and adjust as your passions evolve.

In this chapter, it's time to ask the big question:

What's next?

This chapter is about taking everything you've learned and applying it to the rest of your life. Your journey doesn't stop here. It's an ongoing growth, exploration, and alignment process. Now that you've unlocked the power of your multi-passionate nature, you can continue to create a life rich in meaning, full of creativity, and aligned with your most profound purpose. Let's dive into how you

can move forward, remain connected to your passions, and keep living with intention.

Step 1: Keep Evolving

The journey of a multi-passionate person is never static. As you progress, new interests will arise, and old ones may fade or evolve into something different. The key to thriving is to keep growing. Never feel like you have to settle or stick with one thing forever. You can follow your curiosity, pivot when needed, and allow your passions to lead you in new directions.

Embrace this constant evolution. Rather than perceiving change as a disruption, view it as a natural component of your growth. Stay open to uncovering new passions that excite you and weaving them into your life in a manner that aligns with your overall purpose.

Action Step:

Open the Door to New Interests: Make it a point to regularly explore new passions or revisit old ones with a fresh perspective. Dedicate time each month to either try something new or dive deeper into a hobby that calls to you. Trust that each new exploration will enrich your life.

Outcome:

By keeping an open mind and allowing your passions to evolve, you can keep your life dynamic and ensure you're always moving forward, aligning with what brings you joy.

Step 2: Revisit Your Vision

As you evolve, revisiting your vision for your life is essential. The vision you created at the beginning of this journey has likely shifted as you've explored and grown, and that's a good thing. Your vision is meant to be a living, breathing guide—not a rigid plan. As you move forward, reflect on how your vision has changed and adjust it to reflect your current desires.

This vision serves as your North Star, guiding you as you navigate your passions and purpose. Revisit it often to ensure that your actions, projects, and goals are aligned with what you truly want from life.

Action Step:

Vision Reflection: Review the vision you created earlier in this journey. What has changed? What new elements should you include? Write an updated version that captures your current position and future aspirations. Post it somewhere visible to remind yourself of your goals.

Outcome:

By revisiting and updating your vision regularly, you stay aligned with your evolving desires and passions. This clarity ensures that your path remains intentional and purpose-driven, no matter how much it changes.

Step 3: Take Consistent Aligned Action

One of the most important things you can do moving forward is to take consistent, aligned action. You've learned to prioritise your passions, organise your time, and reflect on what's working. Now, it's about showing up for yourself consistently. It's not about doing everything at once or achieving perfection; it's about making small, intentional steps that move you closer to the life you envision.

Consistency doesn't mean you need to work on every passion every day. It means you commit to making progress, however small, on what aligns most with your current priorities—these small actions compound over time, leading to significant results.

Action Step:

Create a Progress Plan: Choose one or two passions to focus on over the coming month and establish small, achievable goals for each. Break these goals into manageable weekly or daily tasks. The key is consistency—whether you commit to 15 minutes each day or a few hours each week, make a plan and stick to it.

Outcome:

You'll steadily move closer to your goals by consistently aligning actions without feeling overwhelmed. This approach keeps you grounded in the present while ensuring that you're always progressing toward your bigger vision.

Step 4: Stay Connected to Your Why

Stay connected to your why as you move forward—the deeper purpose that drives you. Why do your passions matter to you? What impact do you want to have on the world or your life through them? Understanding your why helps you remain motivated when challenges arise and keeps you focused on what truly matters.

Whenever you feel uncertain or overwhelmed, return to your why. Your why is your anchor when life is filled with distractions and competing demands. It reminds you of the bigger picture and helps you stay aligned with your purpose, even when the journey gets tough.

Action Step:

Define Your Why: Take a few minutes to explain why your passions matter. What do they provide you? How do they fulfil you? Keep this list handy so you can easily refer to it when you need a reminder of what drives your journey.

Define further: Once you have your answer, ask why it is important to me. Do this as many times as you can.

Outcome:

Connecting with your why helps you maintain clarity and motivation, even through doubt or difficulty. This connection also gives you the resilience to pursue your passions with intention and purpose.

EXAMPLE: My why for writing this book.

My "why" is *transformation.* I want to prevent others from feeling the same disappointment and misalignment I once did and live a life filled with joy, creativity, and *personal accomplishment* is possible.

Why is personal accomplishment important? Participating in activities that align with my interests brings joy and *satisfaction.*

Why does satisfaction matter? Happiness and satisfaction enhance mental and physical health while reducing *stress levels.*

Why reduce stress? Lower stress levels allow me to perform better, leading to more incredible achievements and a more *balanced life*.

Why is a balanced life meaningful? A balanced life prevents *burnout and sustains motivation*.

Why is avoiding burnout critical? When motivated and not burnt out, I can continue to grow and learn, *adapt to changes*, and face new challenges positively.

Why is adapting to changes necessary? Adapting to change helps me seize opportunities and overcome potential obstacles, which leads to innovation and *continuous improvement*.

Why is continuous improvement important? It leads to fulfilling my potential and contributing to society. I can achieve my best and inspire others by constantly innovating and improving.

Step 5: Embrace Flexibility and Flow

Ultimately, embracing flexibility and flow is essential to creating a life that aligns with your passions. Life is full of unexpected changes, and your passions will fluctuate over time. Some seasons will highlight specific interests, while others may present opportunities for new explorations. The key is to stay adaptable and allow your journey to unfold naturally.

Rigid expectations can lead to frustration, especially for someone with multiple passions. Instead, practice letting go of the need for everything to be perfectly balanced. Trust that you'll know when to pivot, when to push forward, and when to pause. Embracing this flow lets you navigate life's changes gracefully and confidently.

Action Step:

Check-in with Yourself: Set aside monthly time to assess your energy and passions. Are you feeling balanced? Do you need to shift your focus? Use this time to adjust your schedule or goals based on your feelings.

Outcome:

By embracing flexibility and flow, you'll feel more at peace with the natural rhythms of your multi-passionate life. This approach allows you to adapt without guilt or frustration, trusting that each journey phase has value.

Living Aligned with Passion and Purpose

As you transition into the next phase of your multi-passionate journey, remember that your life is a canvas, and you are the artist. You can paint it with as many colours and textures as you wish. Living in alignment with your passions and purpose isn't about fitting into a predetermined mould—it's about creating a life that reflects the full spectrum of who you are.

You've learned to explore your interests, prioritise what matters, weave your passions together, reflect on your progress, and empower yourself to live authentically. It's time to continue applying these lessons, knowing your journey is unique, dynamic, and ever-evolving.

What's next for you is entirely up to you. You possess the tools to create a life that aligns with your heart's deepest desires. Whether pursuing multiple projects, deepening a passion, or exploring something entirely new, trust that you're on the right path. Your multi-passionate nature is a gift that brings richness, creativity, and fulfilment to everything you do.

Final Thought: As you continue building a life that aligns with your passions, remember to enjoy the journey. Celebrate the progress you've made, the lessons you've learned, and the adventures that lie ahead. Your passions are your compass, guiding you to places you never thought possible. Keep exploring, evolving, and, most importantly, live in alignment with the beautiful, multi-dimensional person you are.

I AM ENRICHED BY THE VARIETY OF MY PURSUITS

Chapter 12

OVERCOMING CHALLENGES

Strategies for Thriving

While being multi-passionate is an incredibly fulfilling way to live, it comes with unique challenges. The excitement of having many interests can sometimes overwhelm, cause indecision, or cause feeling scattered. You may also face external pressures from society or loved ones who don't always understand your need to explore multiple passions—the key to thriving as a multi-passionate person is learning to manage these challenges and stay authentic.

This chapter will examine strategies for overcoming common hurdles faced by multi-passionate individuals. These strategies extend beyond our previous discussions and will provide practical tools to navigate the complexities of living a multi-passionate life with ease, focus, and confidence.

Challenge 1:

Feeling Overwhelmed by Too Many Interests

One of the most common challenges multi-passionate people face is feeling overwhelmed—the sense that there's too much to explore and not enough time to pursue everything. It's easy to get excited about new passions and projects, but that enthusiasm can quickly lead to stress if you try to take on too much all at once.

Strategy:

The "Season of Focus" Approach

To overcome overwhelm, try using the Season of Focus approach. Instead of pursuing all your passions simultaneously, dedicate specific periods—a few weeks, a month, or even a season—to focusing on just one or two passions. During this time, give your full attention to those selected passions, knowing that your other interests will have their turn in the future.

To implement: Select a few passions to focus on for the next month or quarter. Develop a plan to engage with these passions during this period regularly, and note when you'll return to your other interests. This approach enables you to explore specific passions more deeply while reducing the stress of managing everything simultaneously.

Outcome: By narrowing your focus for a set period, you'll reduce the feeling of overwhelm. This approach allows you to make meaningful progress on your passions without abandoning your other interests.

Challenge 2:

Difficulty Making Decisions or Choosing a Path

Decision-making can be tricky for a multi-passionate person. You may feel pulled in different directions and struggle to choose which path to follow, especially when passionate about multiple things. This indecision can lead to procrastination or stagnation.

Strategy:

The "Test-and-Learn" Method

Rather than feeling pressured to make a definitive choice about your path, consider adopting the Test-and-Learn method. This strategy encourages you to test various passions or projects on a smaller scale before dedicating yourself to a long-term direction. The aim is to gain insights into what resonates most with you, enabling you to make decisions based on experience rather than assumptions.

How to Implement: Choose one or two passions you want to explore more deeply. Create a small project or experiment related to each passion to test it out quickly. For example, if you're passionate about photography and writing, you might start a mini photo series or begin a blog for 30 days. At the end of the trial, assess what you've discovered about your level of engagement and fulfilment.

Outcome: This method helps you clarify your passions by testing them in the real world, reducing the pressure to make a permanent decision. You'll feel empowered to make choices based on experience, allowing you to follow paths that genuinely excite you.

Challenge 3:

Fear of Being "Not Good Enough" or Incomplete

Multi-passionate individuals often struggle with the fear of not being good enough in any single area. Because your time and energy are spread across various interests, it's easy to worry that you lack the skills of specialists who commit to just one field. This self-doubt can prevent you from pursuing your passions wholeheartedly.

Strategy:

Embrace the "Generalist Advantage"

Instead of seeing your diverse skill set as a limitation, view it as a significant advantage. Generalists with broad knowledge across various areas often excel because they can connect ideas, solve problems creatively, and adapt to new situations more swiftly than specialists. You can build confidence in your unique abilities by emphasising the strengths of being a generalist.

How to Implement: List the skills, insights, and strengths you've gained from each of your passions. Look for connections between them—how have your various experiences helped you develop a more comprehensive perspective? Remember that being multi-passionate allows you to see the bigger picture and solve problems creatively.

Outcome: By embracing the generalist advantage, you'll shift your mindset from self-doubt to empowerment. You'll recognise that your diverse passions make you more adaptable, creative, and resourceful—qualities specialists may not have.

Challenge 4:

Balancing Structure with Freedom

Multi-passionate people often struggle to find the right balance between structure and freedom. While structure helps you stay organised and productive, too much of it can feel restrictive, especially if you thrive on spontaneity and exploration. On the other hand, too much freedom can lead to chaos and a lack of direction.

Strategy:

Flexible Planning with Buffer Days

To strike the right balance, use flexible planning alongside buffer days. Flexible planning allows you to set goals and manage your time without over-scheduling, while buffer days provide space for unstructured exploration or rest. This balance helps maintain productivity while allowing for creativity and spontaneity.

How to Implement: Plan your week by blocking time for your top priorities or key projects, but leave one or two "buffer days" where you have no fixed commitments. Use these buffer days to dive into whatever passion feels most exciting or take a break if needed. This gives you structure during the week but allows flexibility and freedom when required.

Outcome: Flexible planning with buffer days helps you stay productive without feeling confined by a rigid schedule. It balances structure and creativity, allowing you to pursue your passions while avoiding burnout.

Challenge 5:

Managing Transitions Between Passions

Another challenge for multi-passionate people is transitioning between different passions or projects. Switching gears between interests can sometimes create friction, especially if you struggle to maintain focus or energy as you shift from one passion to another.

Strategy:

Create "Transition Rituals"

Implement transition rituals that help you shift your focus and mindset for smoother transitions between passions. These rituals serve as a mental reset, enabling you to leave one passion behind and fully engage in the next. Whether taking a short walk, practising meditation, or organising your workspace, transition rituals foster a sense of closure and readiness for the upcoming task.

How to Implement: Choose a simple transition ritual that works for you. For example, after finishing a writing session, you might take a 10-minute break to clear your mind before starting your next project. You could also create a physical transition by moving to a different workspace for your next activity. Experiment with varying rituals until you find one that helps you shift gears smoothly.

Outcome: Transition rituals facilitate switching between different passions without losing focus or feeling scattered. They foster a sense of flow and rhythm in your day and help you fully engage with each passion as it arises.

The Power of Strategic Adaptation

Living as a multi-passionate person comes with challenges, but these strategies can help you navigate them gracefully and confidently. Whether you manage to overwhelm, embrace your generalist advantage, or find a balance between structure and freedom, these strategies empower you to thrive as a multi-passionate individual.

Remember, challenges are part of the journey, but with the right tools, you can overcome them and continue living a life that honours your diverse passions and interests. Every challenge you encounter is an opportunity to grow, adapt, and enhance your ability to pursue multiple fulfilling passions that align with your true self.

I AM
EMPOWERED
BY MY
CURIOSITY
AND
MY DESIRE
TO KEEP
LEARNING

Chapter 13

COMMUNITY AND SUPPORT

Finding Your Tribe and a Network of Empowerment.

Being multi-passionate is a unique and vibrant way to live, but it's not a journey to be taken alone. Community is one of the most powerful tools for thriving as a multi-passionate individual. Finding and surrounding yourself with the right people—those who support and understand your diverse interests—creates a support system that fosters your growth and amplifies your success.

This chapter will explore the significance of developing a supportive community, discovering your tribe, and connecting with like-minded individuals. Whether through joining local groups, attending workshops, or engaging online, surrounding yourself with people who appreciate your multi-passionate nature will inspire, challenge, and uplift you.

Together, we will examine how to nurture relationships that enable you to thrive personally and professionally.

Why Community Matters for Multi-Passionate People

As someone with many passions, you've likely met people who don't understand or appreciate your diverse interests. Society often celebrates the specialist—the individual who has mastered one skill or field—which can leave multi-passionate people feeling isolated or misunderstood. That's why building a community of like-minded individuals is so important.

A community offers validation, keeps you motivated, and provides practical support as you work toward your goals. When surrounded by people who understand your diverse interests, you're more likely to feel confident pursuing multiple passions without the pressure to fit into a single box. A community gives you a safe space to share your ideas, learn from others, and collaborate in ways that expand your horizons.

Step 1: Find Your Tribe

The first step in building a supportive network is to find your tribe—those who understand and resonate with your multi-passionate nature. Your tribe may include fellow multi-passionate individuals, creative thinkers, entrepreneurs, or anyone who values personal growth and exploration. Finding your tribe means connecting with people who share your mindset and encouraging you as you navigate your journey.

Begin by seeking out individuals who embrace curiosity and creativity. These people won't attempt to fit you into a mould or question your eagerness to explore various interests. Your community includes those who honour your journey and are thrilled to join you as you uncover new passions and projects.

Action Step:

Identify Your Ideal Tribe: List the qualities you desire in your tribe. What values do they hold? Are they multi-passionate like you, or are they specialists who appreciate your approach to life? Understanding what you seek in a community will aid you in finding the right people to connect with.

Outcome:

By identifying your ideal tribe, you'll be more intentional about seeking connections aligning with your values and goals. This will help you build a community that supports your multi-passionate nature without trying to change or limit you.

Step 2: Build a Support Network

Once you've found your tribe, the next step is to establish a robust support network. A support network is a group of individuals who provide encouragement, advice, and resources as you pursue your passions. These people can come from various areas of your life—friends, mentors, peers, or even colleagues—but they all share a common goal: helping you succeed.

Your support network should be diverse, with people who bring different perspectives and skills to the table. Some members of your network might offer emotional support, while others might provide practical guidance or professional opportunities. The key is to surround yourself with individuals who have your best interests at heart and who are excited to see you thrive.

Action Step:

Expand Your Circle: Consider the people who can support you. Reach out to them and share your goals. At the same time, seek opportunities to connect with new individuals through mutual friends, professional networks, or online communities. Think about inviting those into your life who share your passions and values.

Outcome:

By building a support network, you will create a safety net of people who can provide help and encouragement as you navigate the ups and downs of your multi-passionate journey.

Step 3: Join Local Groups

One of the best ways to connect with like-minded individuals in your community is to join local groups. Whether it's a hobby club, an entrepreneurial meetup, or a creative writing circle, these groups provide a space to share your passions with others with similar interests. These in-person connections often lead to deeper, more meaningful relationships because you can meet regularly and build bonds over time.

Find groups that match your interests and consider exploring new areas. Becoming a member of a local group doesn't merely provide access to a supportive community—it can also lead you to new passions you haven't yet discovered.

Action Step:

Research Local Groups: Look for groups in your area that match your interests. Websites like Meetup.com or local community centres are excellent starting points. You can also find industry-specific meetups like business networking events or creative workshops. Once you've identified a few groups that interest you, attend a meeting to see if it feels like a good fit.

Outcome:

By joining local groups, you'll establish a network of like-minded individuals who share your passions and provide encouragement. This face-to-face connection helps solidify relationships and gives you a community to lean on.

Step 4: Attend Workshops and Conferences

Workshops and conferences are invaluable for connecting with like-minded individuals. These events unite people with shared passions and provide excellent opportunities to learn, collaborate, and grow. Whether you're attending a creative writing retreat, a personal development workshop, or an industry conference, these gatherings help build relationships while broadening your knowledge.

Workshops also allow you to explore your passions more and meet experts or peers who can offer new perspectives. On the other hand, conferences introduce you to more extensive networks of people, often leading to collaborations, mentorships, and long-term connections.

Action Step:

Attend an Event: Find a workshop or conference related to one of your passions. Sign up and attend to learn and connect with others. Be open to networking, sharing your experiences, and building relationships with people who could become part of your support system.

Outcome:

Attending workshops and conferences fosters both personal and professional growth. You'll connect with others who share your interests and can offer support and opportunities as you pursue your passions.

Step 5: Join Online Communities

Online communities offer abundant opportunities for connection. Whether you belong to a Facebook group, a LinkedIn community, or a creative forum, these digital spaces enable you to engage with people globally who share your interests. Online communities are invaluable, especially if you reside where local groups for your interests are few and far between.

Many online communities are dedicated to specific passions—entrepreneurship, personal growth, creative arts, and more. Some are more general, allowing you to connect with other multi-passionate individuals who understand your journey. These communities often serve as a source of inspiration, advice, and support.

Action Step:

Join an Online Group: Look for online communities that match your interests. Whether it's a Facebook group, a Reddit forum, or a niche website, find a place where people actively discuss topics you're passionate about. Engage in the conversation by asking questions, offering advice, and sharing your experiences.

Outcome:

Online communities provide access to a global network of people who share your interests. This allows you to connect with others, offering insights, encouragement, and resources from various places.

Step 6: Collaborate on Projects

Project collaboration is one of the most rewarding ways to connect with others in your community. This teamwork allows you to contribute your unique strengths while gaining from the skills and perspectives of others. Whether it's a creative endeavour, a business initiative, or a community project, collaborating with others can deepen your connections and broaden your horizons.

Collaborating on projects also helps foster a sense of belonging and teamwork. When you work with others, you gain new insights, solve problems collectively, and create something none of you could have achieved alone. These partnerships often lead to lasting relationships and future opportunities.

Action Step:

Seek Collaboration Opportunities: Identify individuals in your network who share your interests and consider potential collaboration ideas. For instance, you might co-host a workshop, initiate a joint project, or work together on a creative endeavour. Stay open to suggestions and discover where your combined talents can lead you.

Outcome:

Collaborating with others will strengthen your relationships and create opportunities for mutual growth. Collaboration expands your network and allows you to work toward shared goals with inspiring people.

Step 7: Create Opportunities for Others

Finally, as you build your community and support network, remember the importance of creating opportunities for others. Being multi-passionate means you possess various skills and experiences to share. By offering your knowledge, hosting events, or facilitating connections, you contribute to your community's growth and enhance your network.

Creating opportunities can involve organising a local meetup, starting an online group, or mentoring someone just starting their journey. Giving back to your community builds a reputation as a connector and leader—someone others look to for support and inspiration.

Action Step:

Give Back to Your Community: Consider creating opportunities for others. Could you host a meetup, lead a workshop, or mentor someone? Begin small by sharing your expertise or facilitating introductions among people in your network.

I AM
FREE TO
FOLLOW MY
EXCITEMENT
AND SEE
WHERE IT
LEADS ME

Chapter 14

STRATEGIES FOR CREATIVES

Thriving as a Multi-Passionate Creative

As a multi-passionate creative, life offers endless possibilities, vibrant ideas, and diverse passions. The imaginative journey is rich and fulfilling, but it also requires a unique set of strategies to ensure that you thrive. Navigating the balance between your interests, projects, and desires can be challenging. However, by embracing your multiplicity and focusing on essential practices, you can flourish in both your creative life and personal well-being.

This chapter will explore strategies designed specifically for fellow creatives like you. These approaches will help you stay grounded, cultivate your creativity, and nurture your creative spirit and yourself. Whether you're an artist, writer, musician, or any other creator, these tips will help you make the most of your multi-passionate life.

Strategy 1: Embrace Your Multiplicity

The first and most crucial strategy is to embrace your diversity. As a multi-passionate creative, you likely have a range of interests that inspire you. You might be a painter who loves photography, a musician who writes poetry, or a designer passionate about fashion and culinary arts. Instead of feeling pressured to choose just one, celebrate the richness of having numerous creative outlets.

Your creativity is not limited to one form of expression. It's a flowing river that moves through different mediums. Embrace the fact that your diverse passions make you more innovative and well-rounded. When you let go of the notion that you need to "pick one thing," you give yourself the freedom to explore and grow in all areas of your creative life.

Action Step:

Acknowledge Your Multiplicity: List all the creative passions you enjoy. Next to each one, indicate how it contributes to your overall creativity and fulfilment. Reflect on how each passion influences your life and recognise that embracing them enhances your unique artistic journey.

Outcome:

By embracing your diversity, you'll feel more confident and energised to pursue all your creative passions without guilt. This mindset shift allows you to explore without limits and thrive in your multi-passionate nature.

Strategy 2: Celebrate the Small Wins

Creativity often involves lengthy processes. Writing a book, completing a painting, or composing a song can take weeks, months, or even years. That's why it's essential to celebrate the small victories along the way. Every step you take, no matter how minor, is progress. Whether it's finishing the first draft of a chapter or completing a sketch, these small achievements deserve recognition.

Celebrating and acknowledging your small wins keeps you motivated and helps prevent burnout. It also shifts your focus from fixating on the final product to enjoying the creative process. Each win, no matter how minor, is a milestone worth celebrating.

Action Step:

Track Your Wins: Keep a daily or weekly log of your creative progress. Write down what you accomplished, no matter how minor it may seem. Review your progress at the end of each week or month and celebrate how far you've come. Reward yourself with something meaningful, whether a creative break, a favourite treat, or simply a moment of reflection.

Outcome:

Celebrating small victories will motivate and encourage you throughout your creative journey. This practice helps you appreciate the process instead of focusing solely on the outcome.

Strategy 3: Trust Your Intuition

As a creative individual, your intuition is one of your greatest assets. You have a natural sense of what resonates—whether it's a project's direction, a painting's colour palette, or a story's theme. Trust your instincts when it comes to your creative choices. You know what feels right for you, even if it doesn't make sense to others.

Sometimes, external advice or trends may tempt you to follow a path that doesn't align with your inner voice. Trust your intuition will lead you toward the projects and ideas that are most meaningful to you.

Action Step:

Follow Your Instincts: The next time you face a creative decision, pause and check in with your intuition. Ask yourself: Does this idea excite me? Is it aligned with my vision? Trust your initial instinct and allow yourself to pursue it, even if it contradicts conventional wisdom or outside expectations.

Outcome:

By trusting your intuition, you will create more authentic and meaningful work. You will feel more aligned with your creative process, and your projects will showcase your unique voice and vision.

Strategy 4: Learn to Say No

As a multi-passionate creative, you will likely encounter numerous opportunities, requests, and distractions. While it may be tempting to say yes to everything, doing so could stretch you too thin and compromise the quality of your creative work. It is essential to say no to protect your time, energy, and creativity.

Saying no doesn't mean shutting off opportunities—it means being selective and intentional about your commitments. By declining things that don't align with your passions or goals, you create space for the projects and ideas that truly matter to you.

Action Step:

Set Boundaries: Review your current commitments and assess which ones align with your creative vision. Identify anything that feels like an obligation or distraction. When you're asked to take on a new project or collaboration, pause and consider whether it fits your goals. If it doesn't, practice declining gracefully while thanking the person for the opportunity.

Outcome:

By learning to say no, you'll protect your creative energy and focus on the projects that matter most to you. This will free up space for your passions and ensure your work remains intentional and fulfilling.

Strategy 5: Embrace Rest and Self-Care

Creative energy is not limitless. To sustain your passion and productivity, embracing rest and self-care is crucial. Overexerting yourself without taking breaks can lead to burnout and creative blocks. Rest isn't merely about relaxation—it's an essential component of the creative process. It permits your mind to recharge, ignite new ideas, and enable you to return to your work with renewed inspiration.

Incorporate rest into your routine to prioritise self-care. Whether it involves a day off, a peaceful walk in nature, or simply taking time away from your tasks, these moments of rest are essential for maintaining your creativity over the long term.

Action Step:

Schedule Rest: Set aside time each week for rest and self-care. This can be as simple as a few hours of unstructured time, a day off from creative work, or a self-care ritual that helps you unwind and recharge. Remember to honour this time, recognising that it is just as important as your creative output.

Outcome:

Embracing rest and self-care allows you to sustain a creative practice that encourages growth and renewal. Your work will benefit from the fresh energy and ideas that arise when prioritising your well-being.

Strategy 6: Keep a Creative Journal

A creative journal is a powerful tool for capturing your Ideas, reflections, and inspiration. It offers a space to explore your thoughts freely, without judgment. Keeping a creative journal allows you to track growth, develop new ideas, and navigate creative challenges. It's also a place to experiment with concepts or jot down thoughts that might evolve into future projects.

Your journal is a personal space, so there's no pressure for perfection—use it to capture whatever comes to mind and keep track of your creative journey.

Action Step:

Start Journaling: Devote a notebook or a digital space for your creative journal. Use it to capture your ideas, dreams, sketches, or reflections on your creative process. Write regularly, even if it's just a few sentences. Make sure your journal acts as a space where your thoughts can flow freely without needing structure or immediate purpose.

Outcome:

Maintaining a creative journal fosters a deeper connection to your creative process and builds a rich archive of ideas. This practice helps you stay attuned to your creativity while offering a space for reflection and growth.

Strategy 7: Stay Curious and Keep Learning

Curiosity is at the heart of creativity. To thrive as a multi-passionate creative, staying curious and learning is essential. Curiosity fuels exploration and growth, leading to new ideas, techniques, and perspectives. Whether learning a new artistic skill, exploring a different genre, or diving into a subject you've never encountered, staying open to learning keeps your creative spirit alive.

Approach your creative journey with a sense of wonder. Allow yourself to be a lifelong learner, always seeking new knowledge and experiences that can enrich your art.

Action Step:

Pursue Learning: In the coming weeks, choose a new skill, topic, or creative medium to explore. Enrol in a course, watch tutorials, read a book, or undertake a creative challenge that broadens your abilities. Allow your curiosity to guide you, recognising that gaining new knowledge will enhance the depth and richness of your creative work.

Outcome:

You will continually broaden your creative horizons by remaining curious and receptive to learning. This mindset fosters artistic growth and keeps your work fresh and evolving.

Strategy 8: Embrace Imperfection

Creativity is often a messy process filled with trial and error. As a multi-passionate creative, embracing imperfection and letting go of the need for everything to be perfect is crucial. The pursuit of perfection can hinder creativity, leading to frustration and self-doubt. Instead, permit yourself to make mistakes, experiment, and create without judgment.

I AM
A WONDERFUL
COMBINATION
OF VARIOUS
PASSIONS
AND
TALENTS

Chapter 15

CONCLUSION

As you reflect on everything you've learned, take a moment to recognise how incredible your journey has been—and continues to be. You are a multi-passionate, creative individual who thrives on curiosity, discovery, and endless possibilities. You've embraced your many interests, explored new passions, celebrated small victories, trusted your intuition, and found a balance between pursuing your dreams and looking after yourself. You've learned to interweave your passions, cultivate a supportive community, and build a life that honours the many facets of who you are.

But most of all, you've embraced the courage to be fully and unapologetically you.

The path isn't always easy. There will be moments of doubt, times when others don't understand your need to explore various interests, and days when you question whether it's all worth it. In those moments, I encourage you to return to the truths you've discovered about yourself: that your passions are your power, that creativity is your lifeblood, and that your journey is beautifully, uniquely yours. There is no "right" path, only the one that feels aligned with your heart and spirit.

Remember that you are enough—just as you are, with all your interests, dreams, and aspirations. The world needs your creativity, voice, and unique perspective on life. You add richness to everything you touch because of the diversity of your passions. You are not meant to fit into a box; you are intended to explore all the possibilities that call to you.

As you move forward, let your curiosity lead the way. Continue to embrace imperfection, celebrate your progress, and trust that your journey is unfolding as it should. There is no rush. There is only the joy of creation, the fulfilment of learning, and the deep satisfaction of living a life that honours the full range of who you are.

When challenges arise, remember that you've already overcome so much. You've developed the tools, mindset, and resilience to handle whatever comes your way.

You are a multi-passionate creative, and that is your greatest strength. So, keep dreaming, keep creating, and keep believing in yourself. The world needs what only you can offer.

You've got this!

I AM
SUCCESSFUL
BECAUSE
I FOLLOW
WHAT LIGHTS
ME UP

SECTION 4

Mapping out your life blueprint

Chapter 16

JOURNAL ACTIVITY 01

Mapping out your life blueprint

Now that you've explored various systems, strategies, and mindsets that support a multi-passionate life, it's time to turn the focus inward. This section focuses on creating a personalised blueprint for your life—a roadmap that aligns with your passions, values, and unique identity.

Through activities and journaling exercises, you'll outline a clear vision of how your varied interests can coexist and flourish. Each exercise will assist you in discovering who you are, what you aspire to achieve, and how to allocate time for your passions.

By the end of this section, you will have a clearer understanding of your path and feel empowered to live as multidimensional as you are.

Journal activities

Find a lovely journal and a pen, and participate in the activities that resonate with you. Please don't rush through them; take your time and reflect thoughtfully on each one.

If you prefer a workbook to guide you, download our Life Blueprint workbook, available from www.maggieoharas.com

Power Questions

The diverse interests and talents that define you are a source of immense creativity and potential, yet navigating them can present unique challenges.

This is where the power of asking the right questions comes into play. Powerful questions spark reflection, inspire action, and foster clarity. By posing these transformative questions to yourself, you can leverage your multi-passionate nature, integrate your various pursuits, and create a fulfilling and authentic life.

These questions will be valuable if you're seeking direction, motivation, or a deeper understanding of your unique path. They will guide you toward a vibrant and integrated life where all your passions can coexist harmoniously.

Consider the following questions and journal your thoughts on them.

Power Questions to Ask Yourself

What excites me the most right now, and how can I pursue it?

How can I merge my diverse passions into a distinct project?

What skills have I acquired from my diverse interests, and how can I apply them?

Who can I collaborate with to bring my diverse ideas to life?

What small steps can I take today to pursue my latest passion?

How can I develop a plan to explore various interests?

What would my ideal multi-passionate life look like in five years?

How can I embrace uncertainty and enjoy exploring new passions?

What lessons have I learned from past projects that can guide me now?

How can I stay organised while juggling multiple pursuits?

What systems can I put in place to manage my time effectively?

Who inspires me to embrace my multi-passionate nature, and why?

What self-care practices can I implement to prevent burnout while pursuing various interests?

How can I celebrate my progress and achievements in my passions?

What new skills or knowledge do I wish to acquire next?

How can I use my diverse talents to impact the world positively?

What fears or doubts are holding me back, and how can I conquer them?

How can I create a supportive environment that nurtures my multi-passionate spirit?

Chapter 17

JOURNAL ACTIVITY 02

Write yourself a letter

Objective: Write a heartfelt letter to your *future self* or your *younger self* (Inner child) to reflect on your journey, acknowledge your growth, and clarify your values and goals.

Materials Needed:

Journal or notebook

Pen or pencil

Quiet space free from distractions

Select Your Recipient: Decide whether you want to write a letter to your future or younger self. Each option offers unique benefits:

Future Self: This letter can motivate and remind you of your goals and dreams.

Younger Self: This letter can facilitate healing, offer closure, and recognise your progress.

Write a letter to your future self or inner child. Start with a heartfelt greeting: Open your letter with a warm and friendly salutation. Use your name to make it personal.

Reflect on Your Current Emotions and Experiences:

For your future self, describe your current situation, what you're excited about, and any challenges you face. Share your hopes and dreams for the future.

For your younger self, remember the experiences, emotions, and milestones from that time. Recognise the challenges and celebrate the successes.

Share Knowledge and Insights:

Future Self: Offer guidance, support, and reminders regarding what is important to you. Share your vision for the future and the steps you aim to take.

Younger Self: Offer reassurance, comfort, and wisdom. Emphasise the lessons you've learned and how those experiences have shaped you into who you are today.

Show appreciation:

Future Self: Appreciate your journey and the progress you expect to Achieve. Recognise your strengths and resilience.

Younger Self: Thank your younger self for the courage, perseverance, and foundation they established for your current self.

Set Intentions:

Future Self: Define clear intentions and goals. Detail what you wish to accomplish and the person you aspire to be.

Younger Self: Reflect on your dreams and aspirations and their evolution. Reaffirm the values that have remained important to you.

End with an Affirmation:

Conclude your letter with an uplifting affirmation or an optimistic message. This reinforces your faith in yourself and your journey.

Seal and Save:

To write a letter to your future self, place it in an envelope and label the front with the date you plan to open and read it.

It's important to keep a letter to your younger self in a safe place where you can revisit it whenever you need a reminder of your growth and resilience.

Tips:

Be honest and open: Allow your emotions to flow freely. Authenticity will make the letter more heartfelt.

Take Your Time: Don't rush the process. Allow yourself to fully engage with the memories and aspirations you're writing about.

Visualise: Picture yourself at the age you're writing to, and try to connect with the emotions and thoughts of that time.

Revisit and Reflect: Periodically reread your letter to your future self to observe how your goals and perspectives have evolved. Reflect on the letter to your younger self to appreciate your journey and growth.

This activity can give you valuable insights into your past, present, and future, fostering a deeper connection with yourself.

Online Resource:

At the time of printing, this website was available for free. https://www.futureme.org/letters/new

EXAMPLE OF A LETTER TO YOUR INNER CHILD

Dear younger me,

You often feel overwhelmed by the many interests and passions that pull you in various directions. You might even question whether you'll ever discover that one thing you're meant to do. I assure you that your multi-passionate soul is a gift and will lead you to a wonderfully fulfilling life.

Embracing your diverse passions will open doors to experiences and opportunities you can't yet imagine. You'll explore various fields, meet amazing people, and develop rich skills that make you uniquely you. Each new interest you pursue will add depth and creativity to your life, enriching your journey in ways that a single path never could.

You'll learn that it's okay not to settle on one thing. Your ability to weave together different passions will become your superpower. You'll find joy in the freedom to pivot, experiment, and grow. You'll inspire others to break free from the conventional expectations of focusing on just one pursuit, showing them the beauty of a multifaceted life.

Your journey as a multi-passionate soul will teach you to trust your instincts and follow your excitement. This trust will guide you through the ups and downs, helping you navigate challenges with resilience and grace. The world needs more people like you who dare to explore the full spectrum of their potential.

So, keep nurturing your curiosity, diving into new projects, and believing in the magic of your multi-passionate nature. Your future is bright and filled with the vibrant colours of all your passions combined.

With love and excitement,

Future Me

XOXO

Chapter 18

JOURNAL ACTIVITY 03

CREATE A BLUEPRINT FOR YOURSELF

Objective:

The goal is to help individuals identify the activities and pursuits that genuinely resonate with their souls, creating a comprehensive life blueprint that celebrates and integrates their diverse passions.

Materials Needed:

Journal or notebook

Pen or pencil

Quiet space free from distractions

Reflect on Past Joys:

Think about the times when you felt delighted and fulfilled. What were you doing?

Write down at least five activities or moments that brought you immense joy and satisfaction. Be specific about your actions and why they made you feel good.

Identify Core Passions:

Review your list of joyful activities. What common themes or elements do you notice?

List out the core passions or interests that emerge from these activities.

Explore Your Current Interests:

List things you currently love to do or feel drawn to. These can be hobbies, subjects you enjoy learning about, or activities that make you lose track of time.

Reflect on why these interests captivate you. What is it about them that speaks to your soul?

Discover Hidden Talents:

Think about the compliments or positive feedback you've received from others. What skills or talents do people often praise you for?

Write down any abilities or strengths that come to mind, even if they seem unrelated to your main interests.

Create Your Life Blueprint:

Create a mind map (activity 04)

Create a story map (activity 05)

Create a Venn diagram (activity 06)

Connect the Dots:

Look for connections between your different passions and talents. How might they complement each other or come together in unique ways?

Write down any ideas or projects that combine multiple aspects of your blueprint.

Reflect and Affirm:

Spend a few moments reflecting on your blueprint. How does it make you feel? What insights have you gained about yourself?

Write a few affirmations that celebrate your unique gifts and passions. For example, 'I am a creative soul with diverse talents that bring joy and fulfilment to my life.

Follow-Up:

Revisit your blueprint regularly. As you grow and evolve, your interests and passions may shift. Update your blueprint to reflect discoveries about yourself and your soul's loves. Use this blueprint as a guide to make choices that align with your true self and bring more of what you love into your life.

Chapter 19

JOURNAL ACTIVITY 04

CREATE A MIND MAP

Objective:

Mind mapping is another way to help individuals identify the activities and pursuits that genuinely resonate with their souls, creating a visual representation that can unlock other interests.

Materials:

Large sheet of paper or poster board,

Coloured markers or pencils.

Steps:

Draw a central circle and write your name or "Me." Branch out with lines for each core passion, interest, or talent. Add sub-branches for specific activities, achievements, or related skills. Use different colours, symbols, or drawings to represent categories or themes.

The example below is a simplified version that provides you with an example. The more detailed it is, the better the results will be for your blueprint.

All the pieces came together when I mapped out what I love doing. I write children's books about travel and create affirmation art to inspire others and make them smile. I have incorporated everything I love to do.

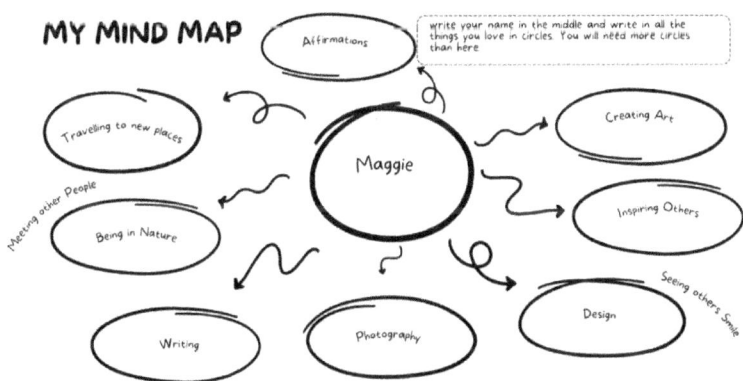

Chapter 20

JOURNAL ACTIVITY 05

STORYBOARD SUCCESS

Materials:

Large sheet of paper, index cards or sticky notes, markers.

Steps: Create a timeline or a series of boxes representing different life stages. Record significant activities, achievements, and interests on the cards or notes. Arrange them on the paper to visualise the progression and connections. Highlight themes or patterns that emerge.

The following example is a simplified version that shows you how to do it. The more detailed, the better the results will be for your blueprint.

When I completed my entire storyboard, it highlighted several overlaps. I could then look at these and work on projects that included several of my favourite things.

MY LIFE

SCHOOL
- Had a vivid imagination
- Loved to write
- Talked to much
- Loved art & science
- Got bored easily

STUDY
- Interior Design
- Commercial Design
- Photoshop Artistry

HOBBIES
- Creating tea blends
- Creating oils blends
- Photography
- Creating digital art
- Writing
- Travelling
- Cake decorating
- Sewing
- Kayaking
- Walking in nature

WORK LIFE
- Banking
- Retail
- Administration
- Design
- Author / Illustrator
- Event organiser

WORKSHOPS/COURSES
- Writing courses
- Spiritual courses
- Art courses
- Personal Development
- Colour & Art therapy

LAST FIVE YEARS
- Written & illustrated 6 x children's books
- Created an interactive affirmation deck
- #01 best seller on Amazon
- Exhibition of my work
- Co-host fluid art workshops
- Taught otehrs how to create card decks

Chapter 21

JOURNAL ACTIVITY 06

DISCOVER YOUR VALUES

Discovering your core values is a transformative journey that lays the foundation for a life of purpose and fulfilment. Your core values are the guiding principles that shape your decisions, influence your behaviour, and reflect what truly matters to you. By identifying these values, you gain clarity on what drives you and what you stand for, allowing you to align your actions with your deepest beliefs.

This alignment helps you navigate challenges confidently and empowers you to make choices that lead to a more authentic and meaningful life. Whether you're embarking on a new project, making a significant life decision, or simply seeking greater self-understanding, uncovering your core values is a crucial step in creating a life that resonates with who you truly are.

Steps:

Create a list of your important values. Use below or create your own. List your top 10 and narrow down to your top 5.

Honesty	Tolerance	Collaboration
Integrity	Open minded	Teamwork
Loyalaty	Forgivness	Self-awareness
Compassion	Generosity	Self-confidence
Empathy	Courage	Friendship
Resepct	Perserverance	Love
Kindness	Determination	Community
Authenticity	Ambition	Harmony
Gratitude	Creativity	Spirituality
Humility	Innovation	Fun loving
Responsibility	Adaptability	Education
Trustworthiness	Flexibility	Learning
Fairness	Curiosity	Balance
Patience	Wisdom	Simplicity
Health	Discipline	Inclusivity
Well Being	Resilience	Transparency
Exploration	Honour	Unity

Chapter 22

JOURNAL ACTIVITY 06

DISCOVER YOUR MISSION

Materials Needed:

Large sheet of paper or poster board

Coloured markers or pencils

Steps: Draw five overlapping circles on your paper, forming a Venn diagram. Label and fill in the four circles:

What I Love: Write down all the activities, hobbies, and interests that bring you joy and excitement.

What I'm Good At: List your skills, talents, and strengths.

What the World Needs: Consider the problems you are passionate about solving.

What I Can Be Paid For List ways you can monetise your skills and passions.

The intersections represent areas where multiple aspects align. The centre circle is your mission. This activity is based on the Japanese concept of Ikigai.

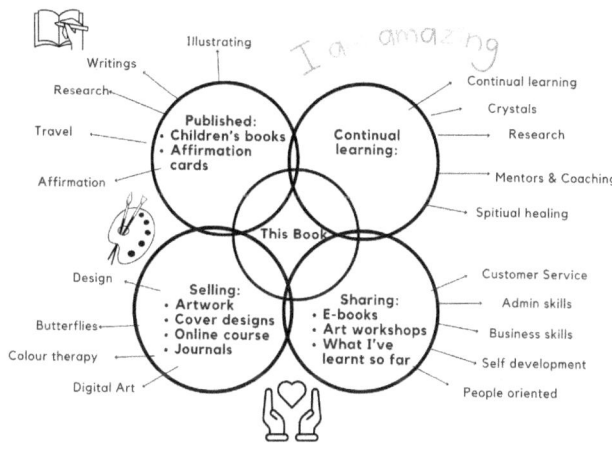

Chapter 23

JOURNAL ACTIVITY 07

DISCOVER YOUR CLIFTON STRENGTHS

Objective:

Using the CliftonStrengths assessment, identify your unique strengths and understand how leveraging these strengths can enhance your personal and professional life.

Materials Needed:

Access the CliftonStrengths assessment, which is available online at *www.gallup.com/CliftonStrengths.* There is a small fee for using their site. (I do not receive any commission or affiliate payments)

Journal or notebook and pen

Steps:

Visit the CliftonStrengths website and complete the assessment. This will take about 30-45 minutes. Ensure you are in a quiet environment where you can focus.

Review Your Results:

Review and record your top five strengths. Reflect on each strength and how it manifests in your life.

For your top five strengths, answer the following:

How have I used this strength in my personal or professional life?

Can I think of specific examples where this strength has helped me succeed?

How can I leverage this strength more effectively in the future?

Share and Seek Feedback:

Share your top strengths with someone trusted. Discuss how they see these strengths in you and ask for feedback on how you can use them more effectively.

Chapter 24

JOURNAL ACTIVITY 08

PERSONA DEVELOPMENT

Materials Needed:

- Journal and coloured pens

Steps:

Describe the different personas you embody. These could be professional roles, hobbies, or personal identities. Think about how each persona contributes to your life. For example:

Persona: e.g., Mother, writer, photographer

Description: explain in detail what this encompasses

Activities: list all the activities that this role involves.

FOUND YOUR ONE THING YET? ABSOLUTELY NOT!

Repeat for as many personas as you can think of. See the next page for an example.

Examples	writer, mother, gardener, traveller, photographer, singer, cook, dancer, worker, friend etc.
Persona 01 Choose one	Writer
Description	I write children's books and wellness and travel articles, journal writing, writing meditations, free writing.
Activities	Writing, editing, planning, researching, marketing, networking

Repeat this exercise for as many as you can think of.

Persona 02 Choose one	
Description	
Activities	

Chapter 25

JOURNAL ACTIVITY 09

PROJECT PLANNING

Instructions:

In your journal, describe all your current projects in detail. Include the steps required to complete each project and any deadlines. These can be hobbies, significant DIY projects, or other types of work. Highlight the three you want to prioritise at the moment.

Project 1:

Description:

Steps or goals to Complete X Y OR Z

Deadline:

Balancing Act

Outline how you plan to balance your projects, passions, and priorities. Consider time management techniques, setting flexible goals, and integrating your interests.

	Goal 01	Goal 02	Goal 03
Mon			
Tue			
Wed			
Thu			
Fri			
Sat			
Sun			
Flexi			

In your weekly Schedule, allocate time slots for different activities. (use different highlighters or pends for each)

Describe how you will combine or integrate different interests into your daily life.

Chapter 26

JOURNAL ACTIVITY 10

YOUR UNIQUE BLUEPRINT

Bring it all together into your unique life blueprint.

Choose a Template in Canva:

Select an infographic template that suits your style and needs.

Organise the Sections:

Divide the infographic into sections: Passions, Strengths, Values, Goals, and Action Plans.

Add Visuals:

Upload images, icons, and text representing your insights from each category. Use consistent colours and fonts.

Customise:

Personalise the infographic with additional charts, graphics, or timelines to represent your action plans and milestones.

Save and Share:

You can save your infographic, print it out, or set it as your desktop background.

Chapter 27

WHAT NEXT?

Now, we understand that we can lead a life in which all our passions, dreams, and desires are acknowledged and celebrated—a life where you don't have to choose between your love of art, your desire to explore the outdoors or your pursuit of wellness. This embodies the *Fleurtopian Lifestyle*, a harmonious way of living that lets you thrive by embracing every facet of yourself.

Fleurtopia

"Fleur" embodies the beauty of flowers and nature, representing growth, transformation, and the nurturing power of the natural world.

"Topia" represents a vision of an ideal place—a thriving sanctuary where individuals can truly live in harmony with their authentic selves.

Together, Fleurtopia represents a way of life that blends creativity, wellness, nature, and connection into a seamless, joyful existence.

The Six Pillars of the Fleurtopian Lifestyle

The Fleurtopian Lifestyle is built on six core pillars that nurture every aspect of your well-being:

Wellness

Nature

Creativity

Multi-Passions

Kindness

Connection

A Life in Full Bloom

The Fleurtopian Lifestyle is about living in full bloom and embracing the chance to explore everything that ignites your passion. It's about prioritising wellness so you have the energy to create, spending time in nature to ground yourself, and connecting with others for support and inspiration. Most importantly, it's about honouring your multi-passionate soul and aligning with everything that defines who you are.

This way of life wasn't always natural for me. For years, I felt I had to choose between my passions or risk being scattered and unfocused. But I realised that the magic happens when you embrace it all—nurturing your well-being, allowing your creativity to flow, and connecting deeply with the world around you. That's the Fleurtopian way, and it's available to you, too.

Welcome to the Fleurtopian Emporium

At the heart of the Fleurtopian Lifestyle lies a sanctuary where multi-passionate women can find the tools, resources, and community to nurture their well-being, creativity, and passions. This sanctuary is the Fleurtopian Emporium—a space to support every aspect of your journey toward living a vibrant, balanced, and fulfilling life.

The Fleurtopian Emporium was created to support multi-passionate souls who deserve a place to explore all their interests without feeling pressured to choose just one. For years, I searched for a space to celebrate everything I loved—wellness, nature, creativity, and the freedom to pursue multiple passions. When I couldn't find that space, I decided to create it. The Fleurtopia Emporium combines what I have learnt, developed, and designed to assist my journey and the journey of my friends.

The word "Emporium" suggests a collection of treasures, both tangible and intangible, designed to enhance one's well-being. From physical products like healing art and wellness journals to digital resources like guided meditations and creativity workshops, The Fleurtopia Emporium is a gathering place to support one's desire to live a balanced, joyful life.

A Community of Winged Sisters

Fleurtopia Emporium isn't just about our products—it's about creating a supportive space where women can unite and grow. We believe in the power of community, where "winged sisters" lift each other.

Through our gatherings, whether it's a guided meditation, a creative workshop, or a reflective discussion—you'll find a space to share your experiences, celebrate your victories, and seek support in moments of challenge.

Our Mission:

We are dedicated to supporting multi-passionate women in living vibrant, meaningful lives by offering products, resources, and community experiences that nurture the six pillars of the Fleurtopian Lifestyle. In the Emporium, you'll find products designed to enrich your journey:

Wellness journals, affirmation card decks, and self-care tools to support your physical, emotional, and mental well-being.

Nature-inspired art prints and meditations to help you stay grounded and connected to the natural world.

Creative journals, books, and workbooks that spark your creativity and allow you to express yourself freely.

Meditations and community practices are focused on kindness and self-compassion, nurturing your inner world and relationships with others.

Your Invitation

The Fleurtopian Emporium supports you wherever you are on your journey. Whether you're just beginning to explore your passions or living a multi-passionate life for years, you'll find products, resources, and community experiences to help you flourish. It is a place to connect with women who understand the unique joy and struggle of being multi-passionate.

You don't have to choose between wellness, creativity, or connection—you can have it all. This is your space to thrive, explore, and grow.

I invite you to step into this sanctuary, where every part of you is honoured and nurtured.

To access FREE mindful colour in sheets and downloadable affirmation cards, go to the website and go to FREEBIES

www.maggieoharas.com

Maggie O'Hara is a celebrated writer, digital artist and creative soul who loves to travel, meet new people and is a lifetime learner.

She is passionate about exploring diverse interests and talents. Her self-discovery and creative exploration journey has inspired countless individuals to find freedom in their passions.

She lives in a charming, art-filled home with her husband and dog and is always brimming with new ideas and projects.

www.maggieoharas.com

Maggie O'Hara
Photographer D. Johnson

Other Books by the Author

Co-Author #01 Bestsellers

Radical Self-Love-How to Ignite Your Light Through Creativity ISBN: 9798858 927891

Radical Freedom- Let Go of Who You Were and Set Your Creative Soul Free ISBN: 9798335 777117

Children's Books

The Elly Rose Journals Townsville ISBN: 978-0-6480513-1-2

The Elly Rose Adventures- Selfies from Townsville ISBN: 978-0-6480513-0-5

Elly Rose in Japan ISBN: 978-0-6480513-4-3

Elly Rose in Denmark ISBN: 978-0-6480513-7-4

Elly Rose in Sri Lanka ISBN: 978-0-6480513-2-9

Through the Door to Sri Lanka ISBN: 978-0-6480513-3-6

Red Sheep Blue Sheep- A tale of diversity and self-acceptance for young readers ISBN 978-0-6480513-5-0

www.ingramcontent.com/pod-product-compliance
Lightning Source LLC
Chambersburg PA
CBHW072004290426
44109CB00018B/2132